I0157829

Money Management for Smart Teenage Boys

A Practical Guide to Strategic Budgeting, Saving, Investing, and Personal Finance for a Secure Future

© Copyright 2024 - All rights reserved.

The content contained within this book may not be reproduced, duplicated, or transmitted without direct written permission from the author or the publisher.

Under no circumstances will any blame or legal responsibility be held against the publisher or author for any damages, reparation, or monetary loss due to the information contained within this book, either directly or indirectly.

Legal Notice:

This book is copyright-protected. It is only for personal use. You cannot amend, distribute, sell, use, quote, or paraphrase any part of the content within this book without the consent of the author or publisher.

Disclaimer Notice:

Please note the information contained within this document is for educational and entertainment purposes only. All effort has been executed to present accurate, up-to-date, reliable, and complete information. No warranties of any kind are declared or implied. Readers acknowledge that the author is not engaging in the rendering of legal, financial, medical, or professional advice. The content within this book has been derived from various sources. Please consult a licensed professional before attempting any techniques outlined in this book.

By reading this document, the reader agrees that under no circumstances is the author responsible for any losses, direct or indirect, that are incurred as a result of the use of the information contained within this document, including, but not limited to, errors, omissions, or inaccuracies.

Table of Contents

Introduction

Don't you wish you could always have money? Do you want to be able to afford all the things you want? The secret isn't just about saving money but *learning to manage it.*

The book has all the information you need to understand the world of finance. You will learn skills like saving, smart spending, investment – and much more that will change your understanding of money. Plus, we'll go back in time and discover money's history, seeing how it changed over time.

Your journey begins by understanding *what money is* and its role. This is important, and you should learn about it at a young age. You may have heard your parents use the word "budget" and wondered what they meant. Well, it's the very concept that will help make you financially independent.

Do you buy the things you want or the things you *need?* You are probably asking, "Is there a difference"? You will discover the difference between essential needs and non-essential wants so you can make smart purchases.

Budgets: understanding budgeting isn't enough. You will be shown how to keep track of your expenses to see clearly how much money you spend every month. You will learn different budgeting methods and find out which is the right one for you.

As you grow up, you should be able to make your own money, right? You will discover different ways to earn an income and the pros and cons of each one. You will also learn to find a job and balance work with studying and your social life.

Managing money doesn't mean just *saving it*, it also means spending it wisely to gain the most benefit from your money decisions.

Have you ever bought something and then regretted it later? You will learn everything that affects your spending decisions and how to resist pointless temptation. These skills will benefit you now. Let's learn some different saving techniques and the essentials of setting money aside for emergencies.

One of the things you should avoid in life is debt. This guide will teach you about the consequences of debt and how to use your credit cards wisely.

Still, sometimes you may need to borrow money. The book explains the terms and conditions of borrowing and how to create a payment plan.

You are probably familiar with the word *investment*, but do you know what it means? You will understand the meaning of the word and the importance of long-term investment. You will also come across the different types of investments and the risks involved.

Have you ever wondered how you could turn your passions into profits? You will learn how to identify your hobbies, interests, and skills and use them to succeed financially.

Follow the tips in this book, and don't hesitate to ask your parents for advice.

Section 1: So...What Is Money?

Money is an integral aspect of life. Everyone knows that even the most basic necessities, such as water, food, shelter, and clothing, require money, but only some understand why. The world has finite resources, which could eventually run out if everyone could get what they need without giving something in return. These resources also need people to extract them and turn them into usable items. Cotton and wool, for instance, have to be found, collected, turned into fabric, sewn into clothing, and distributed to stores worldwide. If you don't pay for these goods and services, people won't be paid to produce them. These jobs would no longer exist, and neither would these goods and services.

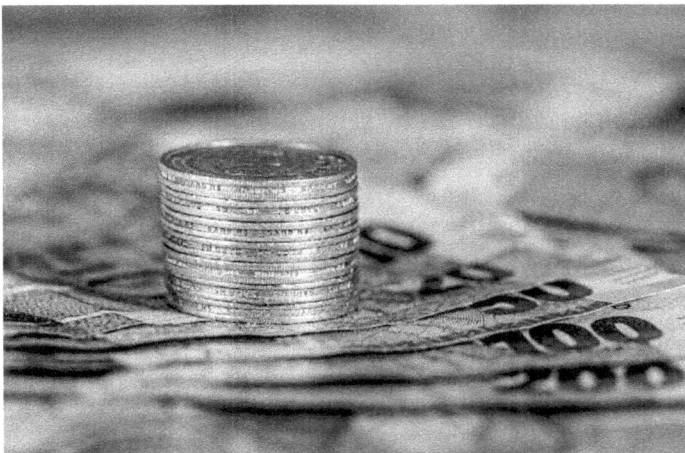

Money is an integral aspect of life.
https://www.pexels.com/photo/assorted-banknotes-and-round-silver-colored-coins-210574/

In this chapter, you'll learn about the importance of money and how it evolved. You'll understand how manufacturers price their products and services and learn about the different forms of money available and how you can use each of them to make transactions. You'll also understand how cash is controlled – how it flows around in the market and how the amounts available affect the price of goods and services. Finally, you'll learn what *financial literacy* is, understand its importance, and how to practice it.

The Evolution of Money

You're probably asking yourself, "Why money?" If you need to give anything up in return, why can't you trade anything you no longer want for something you want? Well, that's called "bartering." People used the barter system from the beginning of time until the creation of the currency system. The oldest recorded use of bartering dates back to 6000 BCE.

In the barter system, for instance, a farmer trades an egg and flour to a baker in exchange for a loaf of bread. In many cases, however, trading wasn't systematic. Since people didn't always have access to the raw material equivalent of what they were trading, they'd have to find something of similar value that the other person was interested in.

The Barter System

The barter system is extremely inefficient for a lot of reasons. It may be tough to find someone willing to trade something you want for something that you have – especially things that are worth the same.

Another problem with this system was that goods and services often had no fixed value. People often exchanged precious items for items that weren't worth as much. For instance, if you were a jeweler who needs plumbing services, what would you do? The value of precious metals and stones is likely much higher than the cost of plumbing services.

The barter system doesn't account for the cost of craftsmanship either. If you give a baker the exact ingredients they need to make bread, then how is their hard work rewarded? The loaf of bread also likely doesn't adequately compensate for the effort you put into collecting all the ingredients.

The Currency System and Pricing

Because of the issues with the bartering system, the currency system was developed. Today, goods and services have known prices and value. Sellers take several factors, such as the costs of business (marketing, manufacturing, salaries, etc.), the costs of materials, effort, competitors' prices, and supply and demand . . . and they use those factors to put a price on their goods and services. Manufacturers factor in all their fees to ensure they break even to cover expenses. They add a profit percentage to the cost to make money selling the product and services.

Manufacturers also check their competitors' prices to make sure their products are priced within the same range. Products priced a lot higher than their competitors' price means they lose possible customers. (Would you pay $100 for a game console when you could pay $50?) Remember: things priced *a lot cheaper* might indicate lower quality.

Here's how things generally work: if the *supply* of the product or service is higher than the *demand* for it, sellers must lower the price to encourage consumers to buy it. If the demand is higher than the supply, the price is raised.

Types of Money and Transactions

Fiat Money and the Role of Central Banks

Fiat money is the type of money you use in day-to-day life. It is controlled by the orders of the government and the Central Bank (most countries have one). Fiat money is a widely agreed-upon medium of exchange. Each country has its own currency that has a specific exchange rate. When you visit a new country, you have to exchange your country's currency for its equivalent there.

Central Banks are responsible for printing money and deciding how much of it is circulating in their country's market. Because of their role, they control the amount of cash flowing between all the banks, households, businesses, and other financial markets in the country. They do this to make sure that the economy is running smoothly.

If the Central Bank printed too much money, the value of money would decrease, increasing the prices of all the goods and services in the market. You've probably heard the term for this: *inflation.* Central Banks also ensure that all banks adhere to the rules and that financial systems function properly. They often lend struggling banks money and offer the government and other institutions crucial monetary advice.

Commodity Money

Commodity money refers to valuable commodities (raw materials used to manufacture consumer products) like precious metals (gold and silver) that hold a specific value, unlike fiat money, which holds no intrinsic value. Gemstones, coffee, and spices are also considered commodity money. These goods held a specific, well-known value, especially during the transitional period between the barter system and the introduction of fiat money, as they were used as a medium of exchange.

Fiduciary Money

Fiduciary money is a more complex concept, as it's purely based on the trust and confidence people have in it, and it has no intrinsic value. It is also not necessarily backed by the government. So, what is it? It's a type of "money" that gets its value from a trust or a promise of payment, like a check or a bank loan. Those don't hold any value in the paper they're written on, but they are valuable because they are "promises to exchange for real money."

Commercial Bank Money

Commercial bank money is what banks have – like huge, super-secure piggy banks where lots of people keep their money. Instead of coins/cash, the bank keeps track of how much money everyone has by writing it down in their system. This written-down money is what we call "commercial bank money." So, when you need to use that kind of money, you can write a check or use a card or phone app (like Cashapp) to tell the bank to move some of your money to your friend or the store you're at.

Digital Currencies and Online Transactions

Digital currencies and online payments are modern evolutions in the way that currency is perceived and used. Digital currencies refer to money or a means of exchange only available in digital notes. There are no tangible coins or banknotes to represent this form of money. Examples of digital currencies include cryptocurrencies like Bitcoin and Central Bank Digital Currencies (CBDCs), which are online forms of fiat money issued by the country's Central Bank.

Online transactions refer to the ability to transfer or receive money using the Internet. Digital wallets are platforms you can use to store your digital currency and make online transactions. Bank transfers are digital transfers from one bank account to another (which can be completed online or through ATMs), and credit and debit card payments are all examples of online transactions.

Financial Literacy

Money affects nearly every aspect of one's life, which makes financial literacy crucial. *Financial literacy* refers to how good a person's financial skills are. In other words, how effectively can they budget their money, manage their finances, save, and invest? Having financial literacy means you have a healthy and intelligent relationship with money, allowing you to start your life's journey on the right path. The earlier you start practicing financial literacy and learning about its principles, the better you'll do financially.

The Importance of Financial Literacy

Financial literacy encourages people to make generally smarter life decisions.
https://pixabay.com/photos/smart-be-smart-clever-mindset-bulb-725843/

Financially illiterate adults usually find themselves in situations such as accumulating debt, financial fraud, and bankruptcy. As you grow up, you'll likely find yourself using debt financing instruments, like student loans, mortgages, and health or car insurance. These types of products are very useful, especially when starting or completing new milestones in your life's journey, like going to college, buying a new house or car, or keeping yourself healthy. Still, you have to know – and stay aware of – how you use them and understand how to benefit from them *responsibly*.

Financial literacy encourages people to make smarter life decisions, avoiding devastating financial mistakes that have a long-term impact on their money situation. Being educated about money also keeps you prepared for emergencies. Financially literate individuals usually have an emergency fund set aside that can help keep them covered for a few months in case of a major unexpected event. Understanding how to manage your finances can also help you reach goals more effectively. You might not be able to afford your goals today, but if you start budgeting now, you can make it happen eventually.

How to Practice Financial Literacy and Grow Your Wealth

In addition to budgeting and saving, adults should promptly pay their bills, check their credit card reports, check their credit scores, and actively manage their debts to avoid getting into trouble.

Next, we'll talk about how to prepare for the financial responsibilities you'll be facing as an adult.

Understand Your Wants and Needs

The words "want" and "need" are not interchangeable. Both words mean very different things, and understanding what each one entails is the first step toward achieving financial literacy. While this may sound very easy to grasp, many people struggle to understand the difference between their wants and needs when budgeting. What makes it even trickier is that needs vary depending on each person's priorities, personality, and way of life.

The most agreed-upon needs are food, water, shelter, and transportation. In some countries, health insurance is also considered a need – if the cost of healthcare services is too high. As long as you have clothes, it's widely agreed that purchasing new clothes is not a necessity. Wants, on the other hand, can include traveling or buying new shoes. That said, sometimes the line between wants and needs gets quite thin! For instance, you may need new shoes because all the ones you have are worn out. However, that doesn't mean you need to splurge on a high-end pair, especially if that's going to put you in a tight financial spot.

Spend Less Than You Can Afford

It's natural to want to create a budget around *the exact amount of money you have.* If you've worked hard for your money, it makes sense that you'll want to enjoy it. But consider setting aside for the future. You've probably heard this before, but adults living paycheck-to-paycheck have very stressful lives! Emergency expenses always come up, and you don't want to find yourself struggling to make ends meet. So, always try to spend less than you can afford. If you move out for college, for instance, consider staying in a dorm. You can also live with a roommate to lower your living expenses. Eat at home instead of going out to eat, and make your own coffee at home instead of going to a drive-thru every day.

Save Money

Almost all goals in life can be tied back to money. If you want to buy a car, you're going to have to save for it. If you want to start a business, you must raise capital. If you want to buy new equipment to support your hobby, you'll have to save up for it. Similarly, most emergencies require money to *get out of.* Whether you want to achieve a certain life goal or build an emergency fund, you have to set a saving goal first. You'll then have to break down this seemingly impossible financial goal into smaller steps. Let's say you're going on vacation in ten months, and you want to save up $800 for that. This means that you'd have to set $80 each month to achieve that goal.

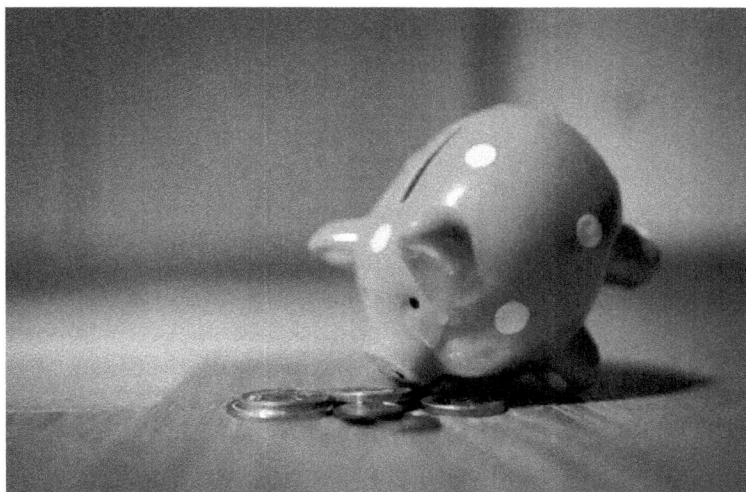

The ultimate goal is to understand how to save money wisely.
https://unsplash.com/photos/pink-pig-coin-bank-on-brown-wooden-table-5OUMf1Mr5pU

The two most used budgeting rules are 70/20/10 and 50/20/30. The 70/20/10 rule suggests that you spend 70% of your income (after-tax), save 20% of it, and invest or donate 10% of it. The latter suggests that you dedicate 50% of your income (after tax) to your needs, save 20% of it, and dedicate 30% of it to your wants.

There Isn't a Right Time to Invest

Investing your money can be a terrifying commitment, especially if you're new to it! You may tell yourself that you have your entire adulthood ahead of you. However, it's never too late to start investing. In fact, it's better to get a head start to make the best use of *compound interest* (something that grows day by day). By investing early, your returns have more time to compound (accumulate and grow), allowing you to increase your wealth. Investing early also gives you enough time to recover any potential losses. You can explore the stock market, IRAs, or even invest in your own business. You don't need to invest a large sum of money; for instance, to start a lawn-mowing business, you could buy a used but reliable lawnmower for $50. That's an investment, too! Simply invest enough to understand how it works and learn from your mistakes.

Build Valuable Skills

Financial literacy is not the only skill you need to learn to manage your finances. You need to learn other skills that can help you get a high-paying job, earn income on the side, or save money in your daily life. For instance, cooking your own food, doing your laundry, cleaning your house, planning your meals, fixing things around the house, and finding the best deals when shopping can come in handy. You can also take online courses or pursue a degree that's in high demand, such as web and software development, digital marketing, SEO, and entrepreneurship.

Have Multiple Streams of Income

Unfortunately, job losses can happen at any time. They can happen in cases of economic downturns, downsizing, mergers, and so on. When you rely on *only one stream of income*, losing your job becomes incredibly life-altering. Fortunately, having an additional stream of income – whether via a side hustle (Uber, DoorDash), investing, a high-yield savings account, or a small personal business – you'll be able to stay afloat when life takes an unexpected turn.

Get Creative

The world is changing rapidly as new technologies and innovations are created every day. While this means you constantly have to adjust to these changes and expand your knowledge, it also means there are always new opportunities to grow your wealth. Think of easy and fun ways through which you can make money. If you're an athlete, you can ask your coach if they need someone to help them coach younger children during busy sessions. This way, you'd be making money doing something you love and possibly establishing a career in it.

This chapter has talked a lot about the role of money and its evolution over time. You should have a better understanding of how to use the different types and forms of transactions – and the importance of practicing financial literacy. Now you know more about making smart financial choices.

The following chapters will give you more ideas about how to grow your wealth, stay out of financial trouble, and control your cash flow.

Section 2: Budgeting: Taking Control of Cash Flow

Are you ready to take the reins of your money and unlock the secrets to financial independence? Perfect! This chapter dives deep into the world of budgeting – your personal roadmap to managing money like a pro.

Budgeting puts you in control of how you want to use your hard-earned cash.
https://pixabay.com/photos/calculator-budget-math-pen-913162/

Why Budgeting Matters

Calling the Shots

Imagine having the power to decide where your money goes instead of scratching your head at the end of the month. That's what budgeting does – it puts you in control of how you want to use your hard-earned cash.

Pocketing Savings

Ever heard of that saying, "Pay yourself first"? Well, that's precisely what budgeting helps you do. By setting aside money for savings, you're building a safety net for your goals – be it a new phone, a gadget, or that dream college.

Escape the Debt Trap

Credit cards and loans may sound tempting, but avoiding unnecessary debt is so critical to your future! With a budget, you're less likely to rely on credit cards for everyday expenses. Dodging the debt trap early on sets you on the path to financial independence.

Plan Big

Do you want to travel the world, start a small business, or be the proud owner of the latest gaming console? A budget lets you allocate money toward those dreams, turning them from "someday" to "soon."

Practical Tips to Ace Your Budget Game

Keep an Eye on Your Spending

Keep tabs on where your money goes. Use a simple notebook or a budgeting app – whatever suits your style. Knowing your spending habits gives you an upper hand in the financial game.

Emergency Fund

Have you ever thought about having a fund just for emergencies? Your budget can make that happen. An emergency fund protects you from unexpected expenses and guarantees you're always prepared for life's surprises.

Tweak and Learn

Your budget is not set in stone. It's more like a living, breathing thing that evolves with you. Regularly review and tweak it as your money situation changes. Learn from your spending patterns and make adjustments as you go.

Budgeting may seem like a daunting task, but it's your ticket to financial empowerment. So, grab your pen, your notebook, or your favorite budgeting app.

Sources of Income for You

Knowing the various possible sources of income can help you understand your financial world better.

Allowances

Regular Allowances: If you're getting a set amount regularly from your parents or guardians, that's a stable income you can count on.

Chores and Responsibilities Earnings: Doing extra chores or taking on responsibilities at home can earn you more money, especially if you're willing to put in some effort.

Part-Time Jobs

Retail or Fast Food Employment: Working in a store or a fast-food restaurant can give you a steady income and valuable work experience.

Tutoring or Babysitting Services: If you're good at a subject or enjoy spending time with kids, offering tutoring or babysitting services can earn you some extra cash.

Gigs and Freelance Work

Online Freelancing: Look through internet directories for freelance jobs in fields like writing and graphic design. Your income can vary based on the number and type of projects you take on.

Gig Economy Platforms: Check out platforms where you can find gigs, like dog walking or helping with events. It's flexible and lets you earn based on the tasks you do.

Entrepreneurial Ventures

Selling Handmade Goods: If you're into crafts or art, selling your creations online or at local markets is a great way to earn money with your skills.

Social Media Influencer: If you have a social media following, you may be able to collaborate with brands and earn money through sponsored posts or affiliate marketing.

Seasonal Opportunities

Some jobs or gigs are seasonal, like lifeguarding in the summer or shoveling snow in the winter.

Budgeting Tips for Your Varying Income

Baseline Expenses

Set up a budget for your essential expenses so you're covered even during times when you earn less.

Emergency Fund

Create an emergency fund. It will be your safety net for unexpected expenses that may crop up.

Flexible Savings Goals

Set some money aside for flexible savings goals – short-term and long-term goals – but be flexible. Say you're saving for that game console, and an unexpected opportunity or need arises. Let yourself adjust how you save, and don't feel guilty!

Knowing where your money comes from and how it can change helps you make smart decisions. So, whether you're saving up for something special or just managing your everyday expenses, understanding your income is a big step in the right direction.

Balancing Wants and Needs

School Supplies

Essential: Basic school supplies like notebooks, pens, and textbooks are necessities for academic success.

Non-Essential: Fancy stationery or decorative items may be appealing, but they fall into the non-essential category. While they can be fun, they are not vital for your education.

Transportation

Essential: Transportation costs, such as bus fare or fuel for commuting to school or work, are crucial to maintaining your daily routine.

Non-Essential: Owning a high-end bike or a luxury car falls under the non-essential category. A basic, reliable mode of transportation is enough for your essential needs.

Entertainment

Essential: Access to educational resources, like books or online courses, can be considered essential for personal growth and development.

Non-Essential: Going to expensive concerts, buying the latest video game, or subscribing to multiple streaming services may be enjoyable, but they are not necessary.

Clothing

Essential: Appropriate clothing for different seasons and occasions is a necessity.

Non-Essential: High-end fashion brands or excessive amounts of trendy clothing can be considered non-essential wants.

Dining Out

Essential: Purchasing groceries to prepare home-cooked meals is an essential need for maintaining a healthy lifestyle.

Non-Essential: Eating out at expensive restaurants or regularly buying takeout can be considered non-essential. It's enjoyable – but not necessary for basic sustenance.

Electronics and Gadgets

Essential: A basic laptop or smartphone for educational purposes can be considered essential in today's digital age.

Non-Essential: Owning the latest and most expensive gadgets, while appealing, falls into the non-essential category. Choose devices that fulfill your essential needs without unnecessary extravagance.

Balancing Tips

Make sure your budget covers enough essential needs before considering non-essential wants.
https://pixabay.com/photos/coins-calculator-budget-101.5125/

Prioritize Necessities

Make sure your budget covers enough essential needs like school supplies, transportation, and groceries before considering non-essential wants.

Set Limits on Non-Essentials

While it's okay to indulge in non-essential wants occasionally, set limits to avoid overspending. This ensures that your essential needs are always met first.

Evaluate the Value

Consider the long-term value of your purchases. Will it contribute to your well-being and personal development, or is it a fleeting desire?

Budgeting for Both

Divide a part of your budget for both *needs* and *wants*. This way, you can enjoy non-essentials without compromising on necessities.

Understanding the difference between wants and needs is so important! By prioritizing essential needs and carefully considering non-essential wants, you can develop a balanced and sustainable approach to managing your money.

Tracking Expenses

Keeping a close eye on expenses is a crucial habit for effective budget management. Regularly tracking your spending empowers you to stay in control of your finances.

Why Tracking Expenses Matters

Awareness of Spending Habits

Regularly tracking expenses provides a clear picture of where your money is going. It helps you identify patterns, recognize unnecessary expenditures, and become more aware of your spending habits.

Budget Alignment

Expense tracking allows you to compare your actual spending against your budget. This helps you understand if you're staying within your planned limits or if adjustments are needed to align better with your money goals.

Identifying Trends

Over time, tracking expenses helps you identify trends in your spending. Are there certain months when you tend to spend more? Are there specific categories where you consistently overspend? Recognizing these patterns allows for proactive adjustments.

Financial Accountability

Recording expenses instills a sense of financial accountability. You become more mindful of your purchases and less likely to make impulsive decisions that may lead to budgetary challenges.

How to Track Expenses

Use a Budgeting App

Use budgeting apps like Mint, YNAB, or PocketGuard. These apps sync with your accounts, categorize transactions, and provide insightful visualizations of your spending.

Keep a Spending Journal

Maintain a physical or digital spending journal. Record all your expenses, big or small, and categorize them. This manual approach offers a hands-on understanding of your financial flow.

Review Bank Statements

If you have a bank or savings account, review those statements regularly. Check for any possible errors or things you don't remember purchasing. Also, this is a good time to make sure that you spent correctly in terms of your budget.

Flexibility in Budget Adjustment

Life Changes and Evolving Finances

Understand that life is dynamic, and your financial situation can change. If you get a new job, experience changes in income, or encounter unexpected expenses, be ready to adjust your budget accordingly.

Regular Budget Reviews

Schedule regular budget reviews, ideally monthly. This practice allows you to see if your budget is doing its job – and that you are, as well. It may help you make needed changes.

Emergency Adjustments

In the face of unexpected events or emergencies, don't hesitate to adjust your budget. Emergency funds can come in handy during such times, and tweaking your budget helps you navigate unforeseen challenges.

Remember that financial management is a journey, not a destination. Regularly tracking your expenses is a powerful tool in your financial toolkit. Look at all the processes involved positively. Be open to adjustments, and celebrate the progress you make toward achieving your financial goals. By staying on top of things (and staying flexible), you'll make informed and responsible financial decisions.

The Budgeting Process

Here's the process of creating your first budget using the 50/30/20 method.

Calculate Your Monthly Income

Write every source of income you have. This includes allowances from parents, earnings from part-time jobs, or any other regular money inflows.

Determine Consistency

Note whether your income is consistent or if it varies. Understanding the stability of your income is crucial for planning.

Categorize Your Expenses

Group all your essential expenses. These are the things you absolutely must spend money on, like school supplies, transportation (bus fare, fuel), and groceries.

Allocate 50% of your total income to cover these necessities. This ensures that you prioritize meeting your fundamental needs before considering other expenditures.

Wants (30%):

Determine Non-Essential Wants

List non-essential but enjoyable expenses. This category includes things like dining out, going to the movies, buying video games, or any other non-crucial spending.

Calculate 30% Allocation

Allocate (set aside) 30% of your total income for these wants. This provides you with a portion of your budget to spend on enjoyable activities and items.

Savings (20%)

Determine your savings goals. This could be building an emergency fund, saving for a specific purchase (like a new phone), or contributing to a long-term savings account.

Calculate 20% Allocation

Allocate 20% of your total income to your savings goals. This ensures you're consistently building financial security and working towards your future aspirations.

Benefits of the 50/30/20 Method

Simplicity

The 50/30/20 method is designed to be straightforward. Its simplicity makes it easy for you to understand and follow without feeling overwhelmed by complex financial jargon.

Flexibility

This method is flexible and adaptable. As your income or financial priorities change, you can easily adjust the percentages allocated to needs, wants, and savings.

Encourages Savings

By deciding to set aside a portion of your budget for savings, the 50/30/20 method helps you grow the habit of saving right from the start!

Tips for Success

Be Realistic

When categorizing expenses, be honest about what truly falls into the needs and wants categories. By being realistic, you ensure that your budget reflects your actual financial circumstances.

Don't forget to regularly track expenses, prioritize an emergency fund, do budget reviews, and celebrate when you hit goals.

Example Calculation

If your total monthly income is $200:

Needs (50%): $100 for school supplies, transportation, and groceries.

Wants (30%): $60 for entertainment, dining out, or non-essential items.

Savings (20%): $40 for your emergency fund or future goals.

Regularly Adapt

Understand that your budget is not set in stone. Life circumstances change, and your financial situation will evolve. Regularly review and adapt your budget as needed.

Creating a budget using the 50/30/20 method may seem a bit overwhelming, but the process is designed to be approachable for teenagers. By carefully following these steps and staying engaged with your financial progress, you're building a foundation for a lifetime of responsible money management.

Budgeting Methods to Consider

There are several effective budgeting methods that individuals can choose from, and the best one often depends on personal preferences, financial goals, and the level of detail one wants in their budget. Here are a few other popular budgeting methods:

Zero-Based Budgeting

How It Works: In a zero-based budget, every dollar you earn is assigned a specific purpose, leaving no money unallocated. The goal is to "zero out" your budget, where your income minus your expenses equals zero.

Benefits: This method promotes intentional spending and ensures that every dollar has a designated role.

Envelope Budgeting

How It Works: With envelope budgeting, you put cash into envelopes for different spending categories (groceries, entertainment, etc.). Once an envelope is empty, you can't spend more in that category until the next budgeting period.

Benefits: It helps control discretionary spending, especially for those who find it easy to overspend with digital transactions.

The 80/20 Rule (Pareto Principle: about 80@ of consequences come from 20% of causes)

How It Works: Also known as the 80/20 budget or the Pareto Principle, this method suggests allocating 80% of your income to necessities and financial goals, leaving 20% for discretionary spending.

Benefits: Offers a simple rule of thumb for balancing needs and wants.

Cash-Flow Budgeting

How It Works: Cash flow budgeting focuses on tracking when money is received and when it's spent. With it, you make sure you have enough cash on hand to cover your bills as they come.

Benefits: Particularly useful for those with irregular income streams.

Reverse Budgeting

How It Works: In reverse budgeting, you prioritize your savings and investments first. Once you've set aside money for your financial goals, the remainder is allocated for living expenses.

Benefits: Places savings as a top priority, encouraging consistent contributions to your savings and investment accounts.

Percentage-Based Budgeting

How It Works: Similar to the 50/30/20 method, percentage-based budgeting allocates specific percentages of your income to different categories. For example, 50% for needs, 30% for wants, and 20% for savings.

Benefits: Provides a structured framework for allocating income based on percentages, offering flexibility for different financial situations.

Bi-Weekly Budgeting

How It Works: This method aligns your budget with your bi-weekly pay – whether that be from a part-time job, chores, allowance, or something else. Expenses are planned on a two-week basis, which can be helpful for managing cash flow.

Benefits: Synchronizes budgeting with your income schedule, allowing for better control over spending throughout the month.

Automated Budgeting

How It Works: Using apps and tools, you can really make budgeting easier! These cover most aspects of your budget, like paying bills (if you have a subscription, for instance), transferring money between checking and savings accounts, tracking what you've spent your money on, etc.

Benefits: Streamlines the budgeting process and reduces the risk of forgetting or missing financial tasks.

When choosing a budgeting method, remember to decide on it based on your own preferences, goals, and lifestyle. Experimenting with different methods and adjusting based on what works best for you is key to successful budgeting.

Deciding which method you choose is a very personal journey. Consider the following things as you decide your approach.

Personal Preferences

Take into account your personal comfort level with budgeting. Some people might like simplicity and flexibility, while others do better using more detailed methods. Choose a method that matches your style.

Financial Goals

Align your chosen budgeting method with your financial goals. If you have specific savings goals (or want to pay off some debt), choose a method that facilitates progress toward these goals. The right budgeting approach should act as a tool to support your financial aspirations.

Adaptability to Context

That complex phrase just means that you consider your current financial situation and lifestyle. If you have a steady income, a percentage-based method might be effective. On the other hand, irregular income may benefit from zero-based budgeting or cash-flow budgeting. Tailor your choice to what's happening right now in your life.

Experiment and Adjust

Don't be afraid to experiment with different budgeting methods. It's okay to try one method for a few months and then switch to another if it better aligns with your needs. The process of trial and error is valuable in finding the approach that seamlessly integrates into your life.

Evolve with Changing Circumstances

Recognize that life is dynamic, and so are your finances. Your income, expenses, and financial goals may change over time. Every once in a while, revisit your chosen budgeting method and be open to adjustments that go along with how things are *now.*

Remember, the goal is not perfection - they are progress. The correct budgeting method is the one that empowers you to make informed financial decisions, provides a sense of control over your money, and aligns with your individual preferences and goals.

Section 3: Earning Your Own Money

As a teenager, you may not feel obligated to earn your own money. While enjoying your last years at school is invaluable, earning your own money has plenty of upsides! Your best bet is to find the right balance between having fun, making money, and doing well in school. While this may feel impossible to achieve, this chapter will be your guide.

Let's see why you should consider earning your own money and how to make money as a teen. You'll find out the pros and cons of each option and understand how to find the right balance between academics, extracurriculars, and work. Finally, you'll find a few tips on how to ace job interviews.

While enjoying your last years at school is invaluable, earning your own money has a plethora of upsides.

https://pixabay.com/photos/money-currency-income-investment-4062229/

Why You Should Earn Your Own Money

You'll Be More Independent

The best thing about earning your own money is that it gives you some important financial independence. You no longer have to worry about asking your parents for money whenever you want to buy something or go out with your friends. Having your own income can make you feel empowered and more independent. You feel more in control of your life and will be more able to indulge in your hobbies, fulfill your wants and needs, and pursue your dreams. While you should practice mindful spending and saving for your own sake, earning your own money allows you to manage your money however you want.

You'll Understand the Value of Money and Learn to Spend It Mindfully

With financial independence comes an understanding of the value of money. When you work for money, you learn how much effort and time it takes to support yourself. You learn to appreciate your parents for not only catering to their needs but for supporting yours as well. You learn about taxes and other deductions that get factored out of your paycheck, which teaches you the value of what you do and earn.

When you start earning (and getting money falls on **YOUR** shoulders), you'll automatically feel discouraged about spending it all on unimportant things. You'll want to save it and spend it mindfully because you realize all the hard work that goes into generating it.

You'll Be More Responsible

Working while you're still in school instills a greater sense of responsibility. You learn how to manage your time and work under pressure as you find the right balance between various responsibilities. This will set you up for success in the future when you have many commitments to juggle.

You'll Learn Negotiation Skills

Working and dealing with money teaches you how to negotiate with people, especially if you're working in sales, dealing with suppliers, or offering services. Even if you're working in a fast food place, you'll find negotiating skills to be useful!

You'll Feel Accomplished

Growing up, you're entitled to have your wants and needs fulfilled by your parents as long as what you're asking is reasonable and within their abilities. If you want something extra, however, it's time to consider working for it yourself. As unbelievable as it may sound, you'll feel *very* accomplished when purchasing things with your own hard-earned money.

You'll Expand Your Social and Professional Networks

Getting a job is a great way to expand your circle and make friends outside of your school and neighborhood. You'll make friends at work and valuable connections with customers, suppliers, and other individuals. Working is also a great way to grow your professional network, which could benefit you later on in life.

Ways to Make Money as a Teen

There are lots of ways you can earn money as a teen. The most important thing to do when choosing a job is to ensure it meets federal and state laws regarding working conditions, minimum age requirements, wages, etc. Several laws are set in place to protect minors (kids under 18) from exploitation within the work environment. Generally, you have to be at least 14 years old to work in a nonagricultural field and at least 18 years old to work in a hazardous environment.

There are child labor laws in America – and sometimes they differ slightly from state to state. Be aware of what your state's laws are regarding your specific age and the number of hours you can work after school or on weekends. There are other legal requirements for minors, full-time students, and those who work under other conditions. Also, make sure to check your income tax responsibilities as a working minor before you apply for a job.

The following are the most common ways teens make money:

- **Internships:** These are great opportunities to gain experience in your desired work field and prove yourself to a potential future employer. Internships make great additions to your resume, too. However, remember that not all internships are paid, so check with your employer whether they plan on compensating you for your work.

- **Work as a Ranch Hand:** In some areas, teens as young as 13 can do farm work as long as it doesn't interfere with their school hours. If your parents own their farm, ask them whether they can hire you as an extra hand. You can also apply to work on other farms if you have parental or guardian consent. Check your state's laws regarding how many hours you're allowed to work on a farm.

- **Babysitting:** This is a very popular way for teens to earn money, but check whether your state has age restrictions. Since babysitting is a huge responsibility, consider enrolling in a training program.

- **Tutoring:** If you excel at a subject in school, you can offer to teach it to younger students in return for profit. Tutoring doesn't have to be solely educational. If you play an instrument well, you can teach novices the basics of playing. If you play a sport, you can ask your coach whether they need an assistant.

- **Car Care:** You can wash and hand polish cars for money. Start by advertising your services to neighbors and make use of word-of-mouth.

Other job options include working in lawn care, the food service industry, retail, or a family business. You can also run errands for people, offer moving help, lift heavy items for people, or sell recycled goods.

There are also numerous ways through which you can make money online.
https://pixabay.com/photos/mockup-screen-smartphone-website-5222446/

As you probably already know, there are also lots of ways to make money online. Working online is a lot easier than working on-site because you're usually able to work on your own schedule from the comfort of your own home or favorite coffee place. As a teen, you're at an advantage because you're likely more tech-savvy and have more computer skills than older individuals. You can use your social media know-how and techie skills to help businesses grow their online presence and market their products or even monetize your own accounts.

Here are a few examples of how you can make money online:

- **Influencing:** You can make social media content that helps connect businesses with their target audience by leveraging the power of different platforms like Instagram, YouTube, TikTok, and even Pinterest. It helps to observe what other influencers are doing to determine what you can learn from them and what you can do better.

- **Social Media Management:** Many companies, especially start-ups, actively recruit young individuals to assist them with their social media marketing efforts. While this is something you can easily grasp through trial and error, consider taking a free online course on digital marketing to learn about the effective use of SEO, content planning, and paid marketing strategies.

- **Freelancing:** Go on websites like Freelancer, Upwork, and Fiverr to build your portfolio and contact clients worldwide. Browse through these websites to determine which skills are in high demand and the average prices others charge. Consider your interests and skills to come up with ideas for services to sell. CAUTION: Do not misrepresent your age or skills!

- **Vlogging and Blogging:** Create a video or written content about things you love and general topics of interest. You can reach out to relevant businesses for affiliate marketing opportunities. You can get paid whenever people purchase something from that business through your affiliate links. You can also earn money by placing ads on your webpage or in your videos.

- **Sell Digital Products:** If you're into art, consider creating and selling an NFT collection on an NFT marketplace like OpenSea. However, if you plan on doing so, learn about Web3 and cryptocurrency and all the imminent risks beforehand. Also, consider talking to your parents before trying this.

- **Online Tutoring:** You can sign up to become an online tutor on several online platforms. You may make more than in-person tutoring while being in the comfort of your own home and working your own schedule.

- **Coding and Programming:** If you're into coding and programming, you can use these sought-after skills to generate income by creating websites, games, and apps.

If you decide to work part-time somewhere, keep in mind that you won't be working based on your own schedule. You'll need to set a schedule that works with school, after-school activities, and any other commitments you have. Discuss what your employer can expect from you, what you should expect from them, and from the nature of your job. Keep in mind that you can't slack off your fixed work schedule and responsibilities to avoid getting replaced. The upside of working part-time is that you'll have fixed and regular flows of income.

If you decide to work as a freelancer or do online or in-person gigs, you'll have the freedom to manage your time and work at your own pace, depending on your agreements with each client. You can choose to avoid hours when you're busy with school or other commitments (like during finals or if you have competitions coming up). The downside is that you won't have a regular or fixed flow of income. You can't guarantee that you'll be able to secure gigs whenever you want to, either!

Finding the Right Balance between School, Work, and Extracurriculars

Prioritize and Schedule Your Responsibilities

To find the right balance between school, extracurriculars, and work, you need to prioritize all your commitments to dedicate the right amount of time and effort to each. As a student, your number one priority should be your studies, followed by extracurriculars and then work. When you get home from school, set aside at least an hour for studying and homework.

Possibly, you could work after dinner with your family, like 7 pm to 10 pm, depending on the nature of your job. If you have sports or extracurricular activities three days a week, avoid working on those days; you can work just two or three days a week. Make sure you have at least one day off from school and work. You can divide your time however works for you.

Choose Jobs and Extracurriculars That Are Important to You

Balancing between academics, extracurriculars, and a job can get very stressful. You already have a lot on your plate, so avoid committing to things you're not interested in or aren't important to you. Yes, it's important to think about what would look good on your college application. However, it's not wise to choose your commitments based solely on this! Look for jobs and activities you're interested in – things that will help you develop your hobbies, talents, and skills. If you like horse riding, for instance, then stick to this as your extracurricular activity and take up a job as a co-coach or a ranch hand. If you're interested in linguistics, join a book club and tutor students.

Set Limits and Respect Your Capabilities

Remember that you won't be able to commit to any of your responsibilities and handle them effectively if you take on too many things. If you feel overwhelmed or feel like all of these commitments are taking a toll on your mental or emotional health, don't hesitate to take a break. There's nothing wrong with admitting that you need time off to recharge. You should also use your grades and your ability to stay on top of your schoolwork as a way to see whether you're on the right track. If you're slacking off, you may need to set your priorities straight and rethink the load and amount of time you dedicate to your extracurriculars and job.

Use Planning Tools

Use a weekly calendar to plan your time ahead. Mark down any important events, tests, and additional commitments ahead to redistribute your time accordingly. Having a visual representation of everything you need to get done over time can help you stay organized. If possible, set time slots for each activity as well.

How to Ace Your Job Interview

- **Know What You Bring to the Table.** Consider how your skills and experience can benefit your employer and contribute to their company. Understand how you align with the job's qualifications.

- **Do Your Research.** Read about the company's history, values, and culture, and verse yourself into its industry. Review the employer's expectations and job description. Prior research can help you determine the critical information to share with your client, appear confident and knowledgeable during your interview, and select questions to ask your interviewer.

- **Ask Questions.** Interviews are not only for employers to determine whether you're the right fit for the role. You, too, have the right to determine whether the job and the workplace are right for you. Prepare questions that will help you understand what the work environment expects of you, how you can expect to grow and develop your skills there, and so on.

- **Dress for the Role.** Interviews are often formal meetings, so make sure to dress accordingly. Avoid wearing jeans, hoodies, t-shirts, sweatpants, and sneakers. Make sure you look professional and put together.

Getting a job as a teen is one of the best ways to enhance your financial literacy and gain insight into the responsibilities of adulthood. Working as a teen prepares you for future success by helping you grow your skills and giving you valuable experiences to add to your college application and resume.

Section 4: Smart Spending

Who doesn't love spending? When your favorite game comes out, you want to be the first one of your friends to buy it, right? If you buy everything you want, you will never have money for the things you need. You should think twice before making a purchase and make choices based on your financial goals.

This chapter explains how to make smart spending decisions and resist impulsive buying.

Mindful Spending

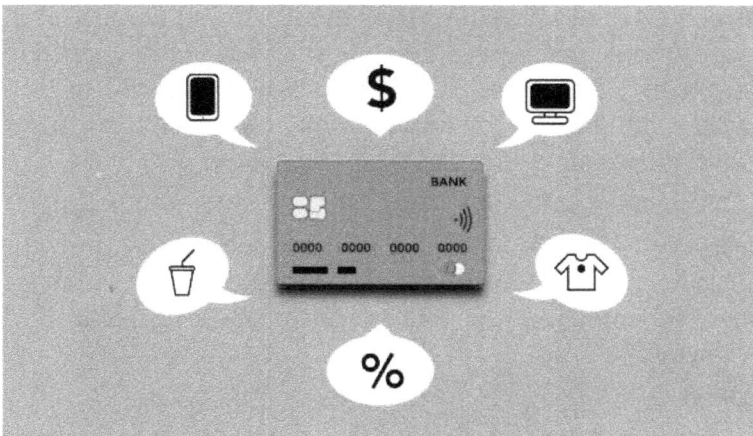

Mindful spending is being conscious or aware of how you spend your money.

https://www.pexels.com/photo/illustration-showing-credit-card-functions-for-different-payments-5849559/

Mindful spending is being conscious of – really thinking about – how you spend your money. Before buying something, ask yourself, "Do I need this right now?" "Is this really essential . . . or is it something I can do without?" Doing this will help stop you from wasting your money on unnecessary things.

Have you ever asked yourself, "Where does all my money go?" When you don't spend your money mindfully, you buy things without thinking. For instance, you go out with your friends, have a big lunch at your favorite fast-food restaurant, buy snacks, and then find a couple of games on sale, so you buy them too.

You go home and find that you have spent all your allowance. If you practiced mindful spending, you would have been more careful with your money.

Everything you buy affects your long-term financial goals. For instance, if you want to save or invest your money but keep buying things you don't need, you won't have money left to achieve your goals.

Benefits of Delaying Immediate Wants for Long-Term Goals

Say there are three marshmallows on the table. You can either have one now or two after three hours. Which will you choose? Many people would think, why wait for later when you can have a marshmallow now?

Most people think the same way when spending money. They focus on what they want right now and ignore their long-term goals. However, it is always better to resist temptation for a better reward in the future. For example, instead of buying a game on sale, you can invest your money and buy whatever you want with the profits.

Self-Discipline

Delaying your immediate wants requires self-control and discipline. You will learn to focus on your long-term goals instead of your short-term ones. In time, you will build healthy spending habits and avoid impulse buying.

No Debts

Do you know why people get into debt? They spend impulsively, run out of money, and end up borrowing. You will protect yourself from debts if you think of your future instead of satisfying your immediate needs.

Improves Your Decision-Making

When you practice mindful spending, you take your time to think of the pros and cons of your purchase. That teaches you to make better buying decisions that benefit your long-term financial goals.

Better Financial Situation

Resisting spending temptations teaches you to spend your money on what you need, save for the future, and improve your financial situation.

Patience

Instead of satisfying your needs now, you learn to be patient and wait for better and bigger rewards in the future, similar to the marshmallow example.

These skills will also benefit you in every area of your life. Self-discipline, making better decisions, and patience are all great qualities that can take you far in life.

Factors Influencing Your Spending Decisions

Look at everything you have bought in the last few months and ask yourself, who or what influenced you to buy them? Maybe you wanted a new scooter because all your friends had bought the latest one. Perhaps you wanted a pair of AirPods Pro because everyone on TikTok and Instagram says they are a "must-have."

Many people and factors affect your spending decisions, even if you aren't aware of them. You may think you need to upgrade your AirPods or cellphone. But if you had never seen the social media posts or your friends using them, you wouldn't have even known you wanted them!

Peer Pressure

Peer pressure affects your spending decisions. You may feel the need to buy clothes, shoes, or electronic gadgets to avoid feeling left out or to impress your friends. Imagine all your friends agree to buy new Nike sneakers. However, you already have running shoes and don't need new ones. Can you tell your friends, "No, I don't need new shoes."? Of course not.

You would worry that your friends might think you are cheap or not cool enough. You also want to fit in with your group.

You are growing up and becoming your own person. You can't go along with everything your friends say or do. Think for yourself and learn to make your own decisions. Always ask yourself if you need or only want this item because everyone else has it.

Remember, the friends who buy everything they want today will never learn to manage their money and may end up in debt eventually.

Social Media

How much does social media affect your decisions? Don't worry. It affects people of all ages. Most teens spend about five hours on social media every day. This amount of time is enough to influence your thoughts, opinions, and spending habits.

Celebrities and influencers have the biggest impact on your spending choices. They use their pages to promote products and make them look attractive and glamorous, so you can't resist buying them.

Say that Mark Wahlberg or Patrick Mahomes promoted shampoo or sneakers on their Instagram. You would probably want to buy them right away without thinking of your budget or whether you need them or not!

You will also find many posts and ads on social media about the latest gadgets or fashion trends. They use the FOMO (Fear of missing out) tactic, making you believe that if you don't buy a certain product, you will miss out on all the fun.

Protect yourself from social media influence by unsubscribing to channels and unfollowing accounts that promote expensive things you don't need.

Marketing

Marketing uses TV, social media, and influencers to impact your spending choices. For example, deodorant or clothes advertisements make you feel that you will look more attractive or popular if you use their products.

They also send their products to influencers and pay them to say how amazing they are. For example, an influencer makes a video about a new game, saying that it is the best one they have ever played. However, there is a chance the game could be boring, but they would never tell the truth because they are paid.

Marketing companies also use social media to target ads to their customers. They show you ads and content that align with your interests. If you love playing video games, you will always find ads and content about them on your feed.

By practicing self-discipline and patience, you will be able to resist market companies' tactics.

Challenges of Impulse Buying

Impulse buying is more than just wanting to own a certain product. You are usually driven by emotions and the desire to satisfy your immediate wants. People usually buy impulsively when bored, sad, or lonely because shopping improves their mood.

Shopping has now become easier than ever. You can just go online and buy whatever you want. When you are having a bad day, you can log on to Amazon and buy things you don't need to feel better. However, this feeling goes away soon after, leaving you feeling guilty for wasting your money.

Many teenagers are still discovering who they are and may have self-esteem issues. As a result, they may end up buying things they don't need to feel better about themselves. They are also more impulsive than adults, so they are more likely to shop without thinking.

Offers and flash sales also influence impulsive buying. They create a sense of FOMO and make you believe that you will miss out if you don't buy now.

Tactics for Resisting Impulsive Spending

Protect yourself from the temptation of impulsive buying by following these tips.

Take Time to Think

Before buying something, take a moment and ask yourself a couple of questions.

- Is this something I need or want?
- Will it bring me long-term happiness?
- Can I really afford it, or will I use my savings or borrow money to get it?

Make a Shopping List

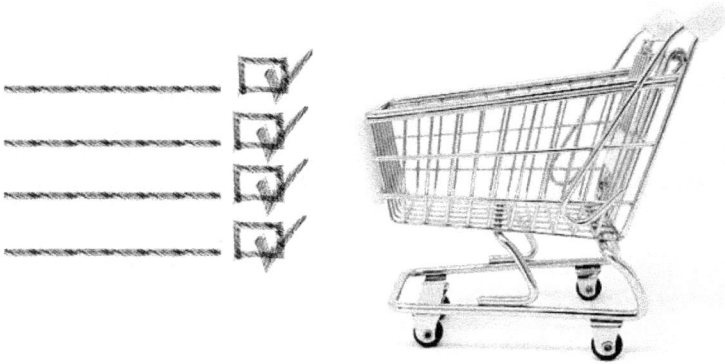

Make a list of only the things you need.
https://pixabay.com/photos/grocery-shopping-list-cart-6507313/

Make a list of only the things you need. Stick to it, and don't buy anything that isn't on the list.

The 24-Hour Wait

While shopping, you may be tempted to buy something that isn't on your list. Consider waiting 24 hours to see if this is an impulse buy or something you actually have a need for. During this time, you distance yourself from the item and can think clearly. You can also go online to research it and read its reviews.

You may find that the product is flawed, or you may find it cheaper somewhere else. Say you find headphones you like. Wait 24 hours and take this time to research them.

However, if after 24 hours, you realize you need it, go back to the store the next day and buy it.

Set Financial Goals

Set clear financial goals. Don't just say, "I want to save money." Be specific. Decide on how much you want to save and set a timeline.

With a clear saving goal in mind, you will think hard before wasting your money.

Avoid Mailing Lists

Don't join many mailing lists – online or otherwise! You can stick to your budget and avoid impulsive shopping for a long time, and all of a sudden, you get an email from your favorite store saying that they have a huge sale. You go on the website and start buying things you don't need.

Don't Shop When Emotional

Seeing that your emotions can control your spending decisions, avoid shopping when you are angry, bored, sad, or happy. You may buy something you don't need just to cheer yourself up.

Make sure you buy something because you need it and not because you are reacting to a specific emotion.

Don't Shop Alone

If you can't resist temptation, bring a friend or one of your siblings with you when shopping. Show them your shopping list and tell them to stop you if you stray from it.

Don't Take Your Credit Card

Leave your credit card at home and take enough money to just cover the things on your list. If you don't have extra cash, you will stick to your list and avoid impulsive buying.

Quality Over Quantity

Always focus on quality over quantity. You don't need five pairs of jeans that will wear out in a year. Instead, buy two high-quality ones that will last a few years. Even if they are more expensive, they are an investment.

Many low-quality clothes won't survive a few washes. So you aren't saving money when you buy cheap. You will pay more to replace them.

Say you buy a pair of cheap shoes for $20. They will probably wear out in a year, and you will have to buy a new pair. If you buy higher-quality ones for $80, they will probably last a lot longer. In the end, you will be saving a lot of money.

Low-quality products can cost you more than their price. For example, if you buy a cheap laptop, it may break, and you will have to spend money to fix it. This can also affect your school work, so you will waste time as well. A high-quality laptop won't cause you problems and will give you peace of mind.

Since you are still growing and your size is changing, you may want to wait on shopping for expensive clothes and shoes. You can still buy high-quality products like headphones or watches.

Simply, high-quality products save you time, money, and effort and make your life easier.

Spending Plans for Teens

Talk to your parents and understand what your responsibilities are. For example, some parents give their kids an allowance for school and going out with friends, while others give them enough money to buy clothes, shoes, etc. Understand what your allowance is for before starting a spending plan.

1. Use the worksheet below.
2. Write down how much you spend every day.
3. Then write how much you spent the whole week.
4. If you go over budget, you will need to make some adjustments.
5. Next, record your spending for another week to see if you stay within your budget or not.
6. Keep recording your spending until your budget matches your expenses.

Daily Personal Spending Record

Week 1	Weekly Budgeted Amount to Spend	$

TOTAL DAILY MONEY SPENT

SUNDAY	$
MONDAY	$
TUESDAY	$
WEDNESDAY	$
THURSDAY	$
FRIDAY	$
SATURDAY	$
Weekly Total:	$ = Total spent for the week

Budgeted amount   Total money spent for the week

What's Left	$

Week 2	Weekly Budgeted Amount to Spend	$

TOTAL DAILY MONEY SPENT

SUNDAY	$
MONDAY	$
TUESDAY	$
WEDNESDAY	$
THURSDAY	$
FRIDAY	$
SATURDAY	$
Weekly Total:	$ = Total spent for the week

Budgeted amount   Total money spent for the week

What's Left	$

Tips on Smart Spending

- When in doubt about a product, don't buy it.
- Spend 90% and save 10%.
- Fix a broken item instead of replacing it.

- Buy used books instead of new ones.
- Pack your lunch instead of eating out.

Useful Shopping Techniques

Save money and avoid impulsive buying by following the tips below.

Use Discounts and Coupons

Take advantage of coupons and discounts when shopping. You will also find online deals on Amazon, Target, Walmart, and many others. You will find big sales on special occasions like Thanksgiving and Christmas.

Compare Prices

Before buying something, search online for its price in different stores. Say you want to buy an iPhone. Check for deals or if they are selling older versions for cheaper prices; just make sure that these stores are legitimate. You can ask your parents to check the website before you make a purchase.

Is It Too Good to Be True?

Say you are online or in a store looking for good deals on Apple watches. You have found a very cheap one, and you can't believe your luck. However, if a deal sounds too good to be true, it probably is. Maybe the watch isn't original, or it's in need of repair.

You need to make sure that any product is sealed before you buy it. You should also check the watch's serial number on Apple's website to make sure it is original. You can also ask your parents to check the product, providing another set of eyes.

Although you should look for deals, be careful, and remember that some can be scams.

Resist the Sale

Shopping during a sale will save you money, but that doesn't mean you should buy something you don't need just because it is a bargain. While the word *sale* can be tempting, if it's something that doesn't fit you, or you don't need it or like it, it is a waste of money.

For example, if you buy a $20 shirt that you don't like and won't wear just because it is on sale, you have just thrown your money away. Think before you buy, even if the item is a great bargain.

Don't Always Listen to Salespeople

Salespeople's primary goal is to sell you stuff and make a profit. They will be nice, charming, and friendly, but remember, they don't have your best interest at heart. They may tell you a jacket looks good on you when it doesn't fit you at all or guilt you into buying things you don't need.

When buying gadgets, many salespeople will direct you to the most expensive ones and usually highlight the benefits of a product and ignore the negatives. No salesperson will ever tell you, "This watch will break after two months." So do your research before shopping!

Make sure that when you buy something, you aren't influenced by the salesperson. If you want someone's opinion, take a friend or a sibling.

There is no denying that spending and shopping are fun. However, if you waste your money on things you don't need, you will feel guilty. Be smart when spending, and always think twice before you buy something.

Section 5: What About Saving?

As you gear up for the exciting journey toward financial independence, there's one skill that will truly set you on the path to success: saving money.

Life is full of surprises. That's why having some savings tucked away can be beneficial during hard times. Whether it's unexpected bills, medical emergencies, or just life throwing you a curveball, having some savings makes you ready for anything that comes your way.

It's your first step toward a rock-solid financial foundation. These savings can come in handy when chasing your dream education, starting a business, or jet-setting to new places. It may sound like something only adults should worry about, but it's a necessary part of money management. This chapter is to remind you that financial security, opportunities, and goal achievement are all within your grasp.

Savings can come in handy when you are chasing your dreams.
https://pixabay.com/photos/money-coin-investment-business-2724241/

Why Savings Matter

Here's a little motivational story explaining the impact of savings on the life of a teenager who is facing financial constraints.

Alex, a tech-savvy teenager, decided to start saving money. Although he is studying in high school, his part-time job at a fast food chain on weekends pays him $12 per hour. Alex starts by putting aside $20 every week from his part-time job earnings. While saving $20 a week might not seem like much, small savings add up!

The Foundation Year

Alex diligently saves $20 every week for a year, putting it in his bank account that pays interest. By the end of the first year, he saved $1,040. Remember, one of the main goals of saving is to have a financial safety net for unexpected expenses – or saving up for a big purchase.

Growth Begins

Let's watch how compounding interest works in Alex's case. Every time he adds another $20 to his interest-paying savings account at his bank, the "principle" (the amount that interest is based on) grows. The $1,040 he earned last year has been growing by much more than just each $20 he add to it, as interest (in the form of pennies and dollars) is being added to the money already in the bank. Let's say his savings account pays 3% interest. By the end of the second year, Alex's savings have grown to nearly $2,400. That's not just the additional money saved; it's the magic of compounding, making their money work harder. However, the rate of compound interest strictly depends on the financial institution offering it.

Turning Dreams into Reality

Fast forward to year five. Alex has been consistent, saving $20 every week without fail. The savings, now totaling almost $5,600, have become a powerful tool. It's enough for a dream summer vacation, investing in a hobby, or kickstarting a small business idea. The small, regular contributions have paved the way for some serious financial flexibility.

The Financial Milestone

As Alex enters the tenth year of this saving journey, the impact becomes even more impressive. The savings have ballooned, showing the snowball effect of consistent, small contributions. Alex now has the financial strength to consider bigger goals like contributing to college expenses or making a significant purchase.

The Future Looks Bright

In the two-decade mark, Alex's commitment to saving pays off big time. The once modest $20 per week has transformed into an impressive $28,000 – when he has only contributed about $20,000. It's the result of compound interest – turning those weekly contributions into a substantial financial cushion for whatever life throws at them.

Alex's saving journey is a testament to the incredible impact of consistent, small savings over time. The power of compounding turns every contribution into a stepping stone toward financial security, opportunities, and achieving dreams. It's not about saving large sums at once but about making a commitment, no matter how small, and letting time and compounding do the rest.

Prioritizing Your Needs and Goals

The two basic pillars involving savings include short-term goals and long-term aspirations. Knowing the difference between them is crucial for a successful financial journey.

Short-Term Goals

Short-term goals are like the side missions in a video game; they're exciting and valuable and only impact part of the game. In real life, these goals are things you want to enjoy in the near future. It can be anything from saving up for the latest gaming console, a new phone, or those wireless earbuds you've been eyeing. These goals can also include outdoor adventures like planning a weekend getaway with friends and much more.

Short-term goals are all about the here and now, making life more fun and exciting. Just remember, while they're a necessity to fulfill, they don't have a huge impact on the long-term storyline of your financial journey.

Long-Term Aspirations

Long-term aspirations are your main goals and aspirations (hope to be, hope to have) that shape the entire storyline and lead to massive rewards. These are the big dreams that take time and planning. For example, saving for college or a specialized course that will set you up for a great career, road-tripping across the U.S., or experiencing the culture in Asia, saving for these adventures takes time but brings incredible experiences. Besides demanding consistency, long-term aspirations require a bit of patience. They may not give you an instant thrill, but the impact they have on your overall story is legendary.

Short-Term vs. Long-Term

The key here is finding the right balance. While short-term goals are tied to the current situation, long-term goals are the ones that drive direction. For example, a short-term savings goal can be something like setting a small amount as an emergency fund or completing a skill enhancement course. In contrast, a long-term goal is saving money to kickstart your business. Furthermore, the long-term goal you set should be divided into several small steps or milestones.

S.M.A.R.T. Goals

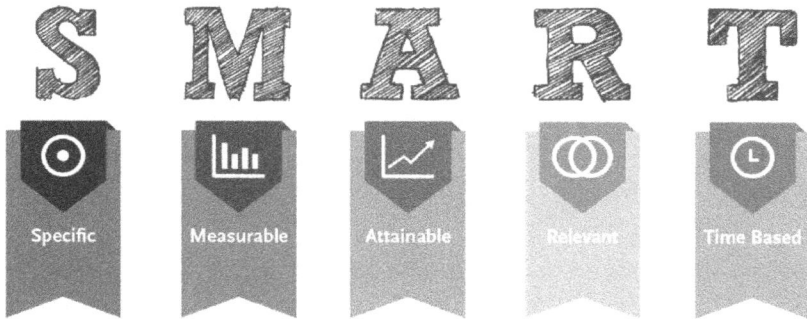

S.M.A.R.T.'s goals strategy is one of the most effective ways you can set both long-term and short-term goals for maximum results.

Dungdm93, CC BY-SA 4.0 <https://creativecommons.org/licenses/by-sa/4.0>, via Wikimedia Commons: https://commons.wikimedia.org/wiki/File:SMART-goals.png

The most practical method to level up your savings game is to start saving with purpose. S.M.A.R.T.'s goals strategy is one of the most effective ways you can set both long-term and short-term goals for maximum results.

Step 1: Identify Your Savings Objectives

First things first, decide what you are saving for. It could be that new gaming console, a road trip with friends, or a college fund. Take a moment to think about your short-term joys and long-term adventures. Your savings objectives are the destinations on your financial map.

Step 2: Craft S.M.A.R.T. Goals

Now, turn those objectives into S.M.A.R.T. goals. Each goal you set should be:

Specific: Clearly define what you want to achieve. Instead of saying you have to save for a school trip, specify that you have to save $200 for a school trip scheduled next month.

Measurable: Make your goals quantifiable. Break it down into manageable parts. For example, setting a goal of saving $50 per week for six months is way easier to track than a vague goal.

Achievable: Be realistic about what you can accomplish. Setting an unrealistic goal might lead to frustration. If you can save $50 per week, that's great. If not, adjust to a more achievable amount.

Relevant: Make sure your goals align with your overall financial objectives. If you're saving for a gaming console but also have a long-term goal of traveling, find a balance that makes sense for your priorities.

Time-Bound: Set a deadline for your goals. This creates a sense of urgency and helps you stay focused. Mentioning the time frame, like you have to save $500 for a new phone by the end of three months, gives you a clear timeframe.

Examples of S.M.A.R.T. Goals

Here are some examples of S.M.A.R.T. goals, mentioning different scenarios so you can better implement this strategy.

Objective: Save for a new gaming console.

S.M.A.R.T. Goal: Save $30 per week for 16 weeks to buy the gaming console by the end of the year.

Objective: Plan a road trip with friends.

S.M.A.R.T. Goal: Save $100 per month for six months to have $600 for a summer road trip.

Objective: Build a college fund

S.M.A.R.T. Goal: Set aside $50 per week for a year to save $2,600 for educational expenses.

Level Up Your Savings Adventure

By identifying your savings objectives and crafting S.M.A.R.T. goals, you're creating a roadmap for financial success. These goals will keep you focused, motivated, and on track.

Saving Mechanisms

Remember, having a solid savings strategy can be a lifesaver in emergencies, keeping you from falling into the high-interest rate trap of credit cards or loans, especially when you start managing your finances.

The following are some savings mechanisms you must be familiar with.

Savings Accounts

Opening a savings account is ideal for short-term goals and emergency funds. These accounts provide easy access to funds, typically low or no fees, and some even offer interest.

Youth Savings Accounts

Tailored for teens like you, youth savings accounts often come with educational resources. These accounts have lower operating fees, higher interest rates, and educational support.

Certificates of Deposit (CDs)

These are an excellent choice for medium- to long-term financial objectives. Fixed interest rates, which CDs offer, are typically greater than those of traditional savings accounts. Nevertheless, your funds are restricted for a set amount of time. It's a wise decision if you don't require the money right away.

Investment Apps for Beginners

Allows you to start investing in small amounts. Remember: many of these investment apps involve high risks that can make you lose your potential savings. Before signing up for any investment app, take the time to explore the pros and cons and learn more about how these investment apps work.

Remember, the key is to diversify your savings approach based on your goals and timeframe. Each mechanism serves a unique purpose, so mix and match to create a customized savings strategy that suits your needs.

Understanding Emergency Funds

What Is an Emergency Fund?

A dedicated savings account for unanticipated and urgent financial demands is called an emergency fund. It serves as a safety net against unexpected costs such as urgent medical attention, auto repairs, or an abrupt loss of employment.

Why Do You Need an Emergency Fund

- Having an emergency fund offers a sense of financial security, knowing you are prepared for unexpected events.

- In times of emergency, relying on high-interest credit cards or loans can lead to accumulating debt. An emergency fund helps you avoid this financial pitfall.
- With an emergency fund, you gain the flexibility to handle financial challenges on your terms, promoting financial independence and resilience.

Setting Up Your Emergency Fund

Determine Your Goal

Start with defining your goal just like you set your objectives. For example, aim to save three to six months' worth of living expenses. Moving forward, list your monthly expenses like rent, utilities, groceries, etc. Multiply this by the number of months you want to cover.

Now that you have your roadmap for the emergency fund, begin by setting aside a small, manageable amount. You need to make regular, consistent contributions, no matter how small, to build the foundation of your emergency fund.

Consider having a separate savings account exclusively for your emergency fund. This separation makes it clear that the funds are reserved for emergencies only, reducing the temptation to use them for non-urgent expenses.

Maintaining Your Emergency Fund

For Emergencies Only

Reserve the fund strictly for unexpected emergencies and necessary expenses. These can be anything from medical bills, urgent home repairs, or essential car maintenance. In any case, if you need to use your emergency fund, aim to restore the fund to its original level as soon as possible.

Regular Review and Adjustment

Regularly review your emergency fund goal. Consider adjusting the goal based on any significant life changes, like starting a new job, increased living expenses, or major life events.

Your emergency fund is a financial firewall, standing guard against unexpected expenses. Saving is a long road where you need to start small, stay consistent, and witness your financial safety net grow.

Savings Obstacles

Irregular Income

When dealing with irregular income, it's crucial to take a hard look at past earnings. Look for patterns, peaks, and valleys in what you've had – and when. This is like understanding the tides in the oceans; you'll know better what to do if you know the usual highs and lows of your financial sea!

Essential vs. Discretionary Expenses

Segment your expenses into two categories – essential and non-essential. Understand which expenses are non-negotiable for your basic needs and which fall under optional or flexible spending.

Flexible Budgeting

Craft a budget that accommodates fluctuations in income. You might make more money during the summer or Christmas holidays. You might make LESS during times you are studying for school exams, going to summer camp, or summer school . . . so make sure your spending patterns match your earning patterns.

Practical Solutions for Irregular Income

Create a Comprehensive Budget

Conduct a detailed assessment of your past income streams, noting the highs and lows. Now, list down all your expenses, categorizing them into fixed, variable, and discretionary. Mark the areas where you can adjust spending during low-income periods.

Percentage-Based Savings

Determine a fixed percentage of your income dedicated to savings. During periods of higher income, increase the percentage allocated to savings.

Emergency Fund Emphasis

Recognize the emergency fund as a financial priority during irregular earning phases and start building your emergency fund gradually, ensuring it becomes a robust safety net over time.

Defining Personal Financial Goals

Clearly define your financial goals, both short-term and long-term. Understand the personal significance of these goals, anchoring them as guiding principles in your financial decisions.

Educating Your Peer Circle

Open communication with friends is key. Share your financial goals, explaining the motivations behind them. This practice promotes understanding and support from your peer circle.

Budget-Friendly Social Alternatives

Explore and suggest budget-friendly alternatives for social activities. Creativity can lead to enjoyable experiences without the financial strain associated with extravagant outings.

Practical Solutions for Peer Pressure

Define Personal Financial Goals

Engage in self-reflection to determine your financial aspirations and objectives. Furthermore, define your goals with clarity, making them a driving force behind your financial decisions.

Educate Your Peer Circle

Initiate conversations about your financial goals with friends and explain why these financial goals are important to you personally.

Budget-Friendly Social Alternatives

Look for ways to cut costs when socializing; you can have fun without overspending.

Competing Financial Priorities

Allocate your savings proportionally based on the importance of each goal. Make sure each goal receives a fair share of your savings.

Practical Solutions for Competing Financial Priorities

Goal Prioritization

This is simple: what's more important? If you aren't sure, then look closely at each possibility, and put them in a list of most important down to least important.

Hierarchy Development

Develop a sort of importance pyramid, placing goals for immediate needs near the top and those for future financial well-being near the bottom.

Proportional Allocation

Now, place your savings where it belongs based on the priority and urgency of each goal. You need to stay flexible and adjust the proportions based on things are they change.

If you understand the basic importance of saving, then you must understand where to put those savings. What's most important? Why? Although it will take some time to get used to your savings routine and cut down on unnecessary expenditures, these steps are a great start foundation for your financial independence!

Section 6: Staying Out of Debt and Trouble

Now that you know how to earn, spend, and save money, it's time to get into one of the hardest parts of money management: staying out of debt. Simply put, when you borrow money from someone, you are in debt to that person or entity. Owing money is far easier than paying it back. When the repayment time looms close, you start thinking that maybe you don't have enough funds, or you tend to completely forget about it. That is when debt management comes into the picture.

When the repayment time looms close, you start thinking that maybe you don't have enough funds, or you tend to completely forget about it.

https://www.pexels.com/photo/illustration-of-man-carrying-box-of-financial-loss-on-back-6289073/

As the name suggests, debt management involves planning your repayments so you always have enough funds and never forget about paying back. It is an essential aspect of money management because if you keep pushing your repayment date, you will get into trouble with the lender.

Debt and Its Different Types

As a child, you may have borrowed a game or a toy from your friend, promising to return it back at a later date. You were in debt to that friend to return that toy. Now that you are older, you may need to borrow money instead. It can be from that same friend or from a financial institution. You will owe the money (debt) to that entity. The different types of debt mainly differ in your reasons for borrowing money. You may borrow different products too, like electricity or a house.

One major difference between your childhood borrowings and teen debts is that you will be charged interest on your repayments (installments). You will have to pay back more than what you borrowed. It may feel like an unfair system, but when you look at it from the lender's point of view, it will make more sense.

The lender isn't your friend. They don't know you at all. So, why would they let you borrow their money? They do that because they will make a profit. It is an investment for them. They give you a lump sum amount now, so you will return their debts with additional increments (interest) in the future. These debts are also called loans, mortgages, and bills, so don't let the different names confuse you.

- **Student Loans**

    A student loan is the money you borrow from a financial institution, like a bank, to pay for your education (mostly for college and university expenses like fees and living costs). It is also called an education loan. A major benefit of the student loan is that you don't have to pay it back anytime soon. You can use it throughout your college tenure and only repay it when you start working in a professional capacity due to the education you gained. The lenders consider it as an investment in your future.

- **Credit Card Debt**

    A credit card is simply a compact card that lets you spend more than you can afford. If you want that new gaming console but your salary doesn't cover its price, you can get it with a credit card. It is more of a simplified system of accumulating debt. It isn't easily available to teens under 18. If you really want one, you will have to ask your parents to provide their authorization. The approval will be based on their account transactions and balance.

You will be provided with a credit limit on the card, the maximum amount you can spend. Say, it's $1000. If you spend the entire amount (say, for buying a gaming console, accessories, and games), you will have to pay it back every month after that, *with interest*. In essence, it is easy to accumulate debt with a credit card, but paying back the amount can be difficult. At your age, it might be wise to put this off!

- **Auto Loans**

  Do you want to buy a car or a motorbike to commute to school – but can't afford it yet? Apply for an auto loan. Financial institutions will lend you the money to buy the vehicle. You will have to pay back the amount in installments every month with interest. At your age, you may need your parents' help to get an auto loan.

- **Utility Bills**

  Electricity, gas, water bills, etc., fall under utilities. You incur a debt with the utility providers since they provide the services before you pay the charges. You will have to pay those bills every month to clear your debt.

- **Medical Debt**

  Unless it's a minor thing, hospitals will cover your expenses for providing medical services on the spot, especially if it's a severe surgery. You will owe a debt to the hospital, which they will send you in the form of a detailed bill you will need to pay.

- **Personal Loans**

  For most other types of debts, you need to provide a reason to borrow the amount. That's not the case with a personal loan. As the name suggests, a personal loan is for personal use. The reason doesn't need to be disclosed. You can spend the borrowed money on anything, ranging from buying your favorite candy bars to purchasing an entire house.

However, there is a catch. The interest rate on personal loans is much higher than on other types of loans, and the time you have to pay it all off is also shorter! Also, rarely anyone gives a personal loan to teens below 18. More importantly, the repercussions for failing to repay a personal loan can be more severe, which brings you to the critical part of accumulating debts: the consequences.

Potential Consequences of Debt Accumulation

Accumulating debt can seem like a harmless thing to do. You can simply take the money or product you want and pay for it at a later date. No need to worry about it at the moment. When the repayment time comes, and you don't have the installment amount, you can just notify the lender that you will pay it next month. It can't get any better than that, can it? Not quite. In fact, it gets worse the more debt you accumulate.

- **Damaged Credit Score:** There is an important factor in borrowing money called a credit score. It's a universal number that is increased or decreased based on your debt repayments. Late payments, high credit utilization, and defaults can significantly lower your credit score. A low credit score can impact your ability to obtain loans, secure favorable interest rates, or even pass certain employment background checks. In short, your future employment options and the ability to get more loans will be significantly decreased if you fail to make repayments on time.

- **Increased Financial Burden:** High levels of debt often involve higher interest payments. This can lead to a situation where a lot of your income goes towards paying off that debt. So . . . you have less in your hands for saving or other expenses.

- **Limited Access to Additional Credit:** With a poor credit history, getting approved for new loans or credit lines becomes more difficult. Lenders may view you as a high-risk borrower and may deny credit or charge higher interest rates.

- **Reduced Savings and Emergency Funds:** Money spent on repaying debts is not available for savings or emergency funds. This can leave you financially vulnerable in the face of unexpected expenses or emergencies.

- **Strained Relationships:** Financial issues are a common source of tension in relationships. Debt can strain partnerships, family dynamics, and friendships, especially if you've borrowed money from loved ones.

- **Legal Consequences:** In cases of significant debt, creditors may take legal action to recover their money. This can lead to wage garnishment (where the debt is taken out of your earnings before you ever see them!), property liens (you can't sell the property because now they own it, too) - or even bankruptcy (which generally happens to adults, not kids).

- **Impact on Lifestyle and Future Goals:** High debt can force you to cut back on expenses and delay life goals like buying a home or car, furthering education, or even retirement planning.

- **Bankruptcy Risk:** In extreme cases, adults find themselves in a situation where declaring bankruptcy is the only viable option to manage their overwhelming debt. In essence, when you are unable to pay your outstanding debts, you will need to declare bankruptcy – which tells the whole world of banks that you couldn't and didn't pay your debt. This lowers your credit score. Even though bankruptcy may seem like a fresh start, it will hurt you in the future.

In short, the consequences of failing to repay your debts can be very severe. Systems are already in place to help you make your regular installments. Pay your debts! Better yet, don't accrue very many.

Emotional Effects of Incurring Debt

If you are able to pay them back in time, debts can have a positive impact on your life. If you keep accumulating debt, its negative effects can be awful! However, they are just the tip of the iceberg compared to its emotional and mental effects.

- **Stress:** This is probably the most common effect of accumulating debt in teens. You are already burdened with the pressures of adolescence and academics. The inability to pay off your debt can cause additional stress.

- **Anxiety:** Stress and anxiety often go hand in hand, especially if the former has reached unmanageable levels. In essence, anxiety is nothing but the physical effect of stress, with increased heartbeat, incessant headaches, and continual shortness of breath.

- **Bouts of Anger:** When you are in debt, you may be bombarded with phone calls and messages from collection agents. Lashing out at them for the problems in your life is a common emotion, though unfair to them. They are just doing their job, after all. These unnecessary bouts of anger may spill into other parts of your life.

- **Depression:** If all the negative emotions mentioned are prolonged due to your mounting debt, they will eventually lead to depression and hopelessness. These are probably the worst emotions during your teens, a time when you are usually full of excitement and hope.

- **Denial:** This is a common emotion found in teens incurring debt. You tend to think that you have your whole life ahead of you to make repayments. Why not have some fun? It's not a bad philosophical mindset, but you are having fun with someone else's money, not *yours.* Don't deny that fact, and pay your debts on time.

Consumerism

Consumerism is buying products you don't need because advertisements and peer influence motivate you to buy them. At your age, it is easy to get seduced by the idea of owning stuff you won't necessarily use just because other people have it and you have the means to buy it.

Imagine that the students in your school group are into a particular PlayStation game, but you don't have the console itself, so you are often left out of their discussions. To feel more accepted by the group, you may purchase the console on credit, leaving you in debt, which you may not be able to repay. Avoid falling for consumerism to stay out of debt and trouble, which brings you to the next section.

Principles of Responsible Borrowing

Don't go into needless debt to safeguard your future, but if you have to borrow, make sure it's for something you need.

- **Needs vs. Wants**

  This is an easy concept to understand but hard to implement. Note down all the things you wish to buy and divide them into two categories: needs and wants. While considering each thing, ask yourself one question, "Can you survive without it?" If the answer is yes, place it into "wants." If it's no, it goes into "needs." Borrow only for those things in the "needs" section before considering your "wants."

- **Credit Scores**

  Your credit score is a measure of your ability to be eligible for low-interest loans and credit. The higher your score, the higher your chance of getting a loan and the better interest rate you will receive. Your score depends on your credit history (loans paid, defaulted, delayed installments, etc.).

- **Budgeting**

  Setting a weekly, monthly, or yearly budget helps you manage your finances more effectively. You know if you can afford to borrow money at any point during the tenure. All you have to do is make a financial plan for your future. Include your income, spending, savings, and any pending loans. Spending should include everything, from gas money to your phone bills.

Common Financial Scams and Predatory Lending Practices

Whenever money is involved, scammers and *predatory lenders* (those who prey on unsuspecting consumers) aren't too far away. They promote an attractive and easily attainable scheme but hide a strategy that may even leave you completely broke in the end. Teens unaware of such scams often fall prey to them.

Whenever money is involved, scammers and predatory lenders aren't too far away.
https://www.pexels.com/photo/conceptual-photo-of-a-money-scam-7111619/

Scams

Phishing Scams: This involves fraudsters impersonating legitimate organizations (like banks) through emails or text messages, trying to trick you into providing sensitive information like account numbers, passwords, and Social Security numbers.

Advance-Fee Scams: You're told you have won a prize, are eligible for a great investment, or have been approved for a loan, but you must pay an upfront fee to access it. Once the fee is paid, the scammer disappears.

Lottery and Sweepstakes Scams: You receive notifications that you have won a lottery or sweepstakes, but you need to pay taxes or fees to claim the prize. The prize, however, doesn't exist.

Ponzi and Pyramid Schemes: These investment scams involve paying returns to earlier investors with the capital of newer investors. Ponzi schemes promise high returns with little or no risk, while pyramid schemes involve making money primarily by recruiting new participants.

Identity Theft: This occurs when someone steals personal information and uses it to commit fraud, like opening credit accounts or taking out loans in your name.

Romance Scams: Scammers create fake profiles on dating sites or social media to build relationships and eventually convince you to send money under false pretenses.

Debt Settlement and Debt Relief Scams: Companies falsely claim they can negotiate with creditors to reduce debt but often charge high fees and sometimes don't negotiate at all, leaving you worse off.

Predatory Lending Practices

These include unfair, deceptive, or fraudulent practices during the loan origination process.

Exorbitant Interest Rates: Lenders charge extremely high interest rates that make it difficult for borrowers to repay the loan.

Loan Flipping: Repeatedly refinancing loans to charge high fees each time without any real benefit to the borrower.

Hidden Fees and Balloon Payments: Incorporating undisclosed fees or large balloon payments at the end of a loan term.

Bait and Switch: Offering one set of terms when someone applies, then changing them or pressuring the borrower into accepting different terms at signing.

To avoid falling for such scams and lending practices, you need to understand there is no easy way to make or borrow money. Carefully read the terms and conditions of the loan you're applying for. Don't make any payments upfront or put up collateral (something you own, which can be seized if you fail to make repayments) if you don't trust the source.

In essence, try to live a lifestyle that aligns with your income. Follow the 50/30/20 rule to avoid getting into debt (unless it's an emergency). Set aside 50% of your income for "needs," 30% for "wants," and 20% as savings. If your wants are going beyond 30%, don't take it out of your savings. Consider changing your lifestyle instead. For instance, you can downgrade from that top-speed internet plan to something you can afford.

Section 7: Investing for Teens

When you have more money than you know what to do with, you may wonder what you can sensibly do with it. The most straightforward answer is to stash it somewhere safe for future use. Are you hoping to buy something expensive? You can let the money sit in your bank account until you have enough. The smart option, though, will be to invest the money so it can keep on growing with you!

Investing - What Is It?

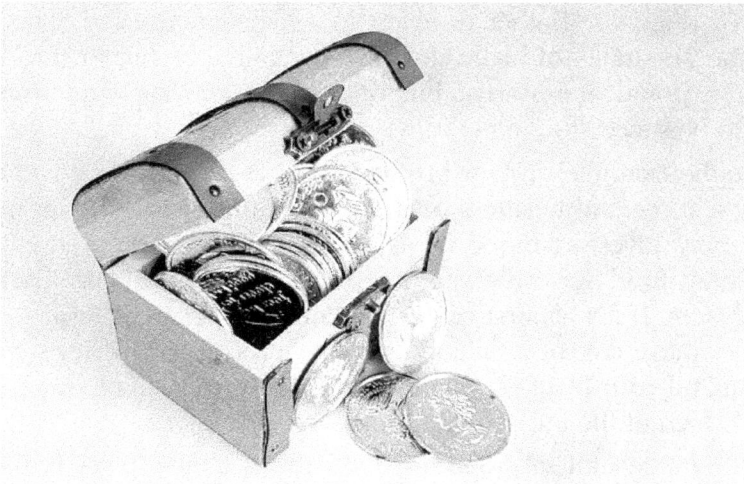

Instead of stashing your money somewhere safe, invest your money so it can keep on growing with you!

https://pixabay.com/photos/gold-wealth-treasure-investment-3146939/

When you let someone else borrow what you own (mostly money), it will be returned to you at a future date along with financial interest. That can be a real estate project, business stocks, bonds, etc. At its core, investing is the opposite of borrowing. In this case, you act as the lender, and your profits are like the interest earned by the bank when you borrow. However, investing is more binding than giving out loans and expecting interest in return. There is more risk involved in the former.

Imagine your brother is starting a new business venture (say, an online retail store). You want to help him by covering the store's initial costs, from creating the website to purchasing the wholesale products for sale. In financial terms, you will be investing in his business. Once his business takes off and he starts making profits, he will give you a part of those profits to repay you or thank you for your favor and as a return on your investment.

At this point, you can choose to keep investing your profits (shares) to help his business grow even more, or cash out your entire investment plus the profits to use the money however you want. That is how stocks and bonds work, but you will get into it later in the chapter. Before you begin investing, it is critical to understand the concept of risk and return.

Risk and Return

When you invest your money, you always risk losing some or all of it. The risk can be high or low depending on the asset you are investing in. Why would anyone bother to invest in a high-risk project? The answer lies in the possibility of high returns. Essentially, the higher the risk, the better the potential rewards, but only if the venture you invested in proves to be successful.

Take the example of your brother's business again. If he was already running a successful business before starting the new one, you wouldn't be the only investor. Since he is an established entrepreneur, many others may fund his new venture, but each of your profits will be relatively less. If it's his first venture, other investors may hesitate to fund a newbie (more risk of it failing), leaving you as the only investor. Since only you and your brother will be sharing the profits, your shares will be relatively high (if the business becomes successful).

There are several safe options that will guarantee lower returns, but you are usually safer if some major calamity occurs. Things like savings accounts and government bonds are ideal to start your investing journey. Higher-risk products that offer higher returns are stocks and real estate.

Benefits of Long-Term Investing

The earlier you invest, the more profit you will make later in life. Teenage years are an ideal time to begin, but do you need to keep investing more and more money to get bigger returns? Not quite. There is a concept called ***compounding.*** We've talked about this a little already (Remember Alex?) It refers to the process where the interest earned on an investment is reinvested to earn additional interest instead of being paid out. You earn interest not only on your original investment but also on the interest that has been added to that investment. Over time, compounding can significantly increase the growth of your investments.

Initially, the interest is minimal compared to your investment. However, as it gets added each year to your investment, say 10-15 years down the line, you will get significant additional gains without making any further investments. Other than compounding interest, the other benefits of long-term investing include:

- **Reduced Impact of Volatility**

  Financial markets can change up or down in the short term, with prices fluctuating due to various factors such as economic news, political events, and market sentiment. Long-term investors don't let short-term volatility because they are focused on the potential for growth over *many years.* Over time, the markets have historically trended upwards, meaning that temporary declines are often followed by recoveries and gains.

- **Lower Transaction Costs**

  Frequent investing (or trading) can lead to high transaction costs, including brokerage fees and taxes on capital gains (that's when the government takes a portion of your "gains" – things like interest paid to you or profit made by selling something.). Long-term investing minimizes these costs because it involves fewer transactions. By holding investments for more extended periods, you can reduce the impact of transaction costs on your overall returns.

- **Benefit from Long-Term Market Trends**

  Investing for the long term allows you to take advantage of long-term market trends, such as technological advancements (think AI), demographic shifts, and economic growth. By staying invested through market cycles, you can participate in the growth potential of these trends.

- **Emotional and Psychological Benefits**

  Short-term market fluctuations can lead to stress and anxiety, causing you to make impulsive decisions that may harm your financial goals. A long-term perspective helps you remain focused on your main objective.

- **Opportunity to Invest in Growth**

  Investing for the long term provides the opportunity to invest in growth sectors or companies that may not deliver immediate returns – but their day is coming! Think of AI companies now; it's relatively new, but investing in this industry could pay off big down the road!

Common Investment Vehicles Suitable for Teens

Does the prospect of investing and growing your money intrigue you? Don't get your hopes too high, though. Only people who are 18 years and above can invest all by themselves. Don't be disappointed, either! The good news is you can still invest in your early teens with the help of your parents or guardians. It is crucial to understand the different investment options before getting into them.

- **Stocks (Equities):** A tiny portion of ownership in a firm can be acquired by acquiring shares of stock. Although stocks can yield large gains, they also carry a higher level of risk since the performance of the firm and the state of the market can have a substantial impact on their value.

  - **Bonds:** To put it simply, bonds are loans made to borrowers – usually by government or businesses – that will later repay the principal amount plus interest. Generally speaking, they are less risky than equities and yield smaller returns.

  - **Mutual Funds:** These are when investors have gotten together to buy a variety of stocks, bonds, and other assets. Professional portfolio managers oversee mutual funds. These funds allow you to invest in a basket of many things without breaking the bank and while reducing the risk associated with ONE big thing.

- **Exchange-Traded Funds (ETFs):** Similar to mutual funds, ETFs are pools of investments that track an index, commodity, bonds, or a basket of assets like an index fund. However, ETFs trade on stock exchanges like individual stocks, offering more flexibility and often lower fees than mutual funds.

- **Real Estate:** Down the road for you, probably. Still, rent from rental properties and possible value growth from real estate investments can make money, too. Real estate investment can require a lot of money (which is why it might not be in your immediate future), and there are unique risks like market fluctuations and property management challenges.

- **Certificates of Deposit (CDs):** CDs are time-bound deposit accounts offered by banks with a fixed interest rate and maturity date. They are low-risk investments but offer lower returns compared to stocks or bonds.

- **Savings Accounts:** While not typically considered an investment due to their low returns, high-yield savings accounts offer a safe place to park money while earning some interest.

- **Retirement Accounts (IRA, Roth IRA, 401(k), etc.):** Planning for your retirement as a teenager can give you very high returns in the future. Retirement accounts are tax-advantaged accounts designed for long-term savings. Contributions may be tax-deductible or withdrawals tax-free, depending on the account type. They can hold various investment products like stocks, bonds, mutual funds, and ETFs.

- **Commodities:** You may diversify your investment portfolio or act as a buffer against inflation by making investments in tangible commodities like gold, silver, oil, or agricultural products. Commodities can be volatile and are influenced by market, geopolitical, and environmental factors.

- **Cryptocurrencies:** You will have heard this term several times since the cryptocurrency boom in the late 2000s. They are a sort of virtual commodity or currency that has a real-world value. They are highly speculative and subject to significant volatility and regulatory risks.

As a teen, you can explore options like:

Custodial Brokerage Accounts: A parent or guardian can open a custodial brokerage account, such as a UGMA (Uniform Gifts to Minors Act) or UTMA (Uniform Transfers to Minors Act) account, which allows them to invest in assets on your behalf.

Education Savings Accounts (ESAs) or 529 Plans: These accounts are specifically for saving for education expenses. Contributions grow tax-free, and withdrawals are tax-free when used for qualified education expenses.

Roth IRA for Minors: If you have earned income from a job, you can contribute to a Roth IRA. This can be a powerful way to start saving for retirement early, as the money grows tax-free and withdrawals in retirement are tax-free.

High-Yield Savings Accounts or CDs: For a more conservative investment, a high-yield savings account or a Certificate of Deposit (CD) can offer slightly higher interest rates than a regular savings account. The returns are still lower than those of the stock market, though.

Learning and Simulation Tools: Do you want to practice mock trading before dabbling in the real thing? There are various apps and online platforms that allow you to learn about investing through simulations. These tools often use virtual money to invest in the stock market, which can be an educational experience without any financial risk.

Micro-Investing Apps: Some apps round up purchases to the nearest dollar and invest the change. These can be a good way to start investing with small amounts of money.

Diversification

With this inverse proportionality of risks and returns, you may be wondering how you can get the greatest returns with the least amount of risk. It's entirely possible, but it requires more work. In the previous section, you came across a new financial term, *diversification*, in the mutual funds paragraph. This is an approach used to manage risk and maximize returns by spreading investments across different financial instruments, accounts, and other commodities.

Stay with me here... Different investment options are associated with different levels of risks and returns, but the overall market is often growing. Because of this, there's a better chance that your diversified investments will yield a profit. You can do it on your own, use specially created tools like mutual funds, or seek professional help from financial advisors.

Risks Involved

While minimizing risks with diversification is a viable option, in most other cases, you will have to learn how to manage risks.

https://pixabay.com/photos/caution-sign-safety-warning-risk-454360/

Before diving into the world of investments, it's essential to understand the risks involved.

- **Market Risk (Systematic Risk):** Economic recessions, political turmoil, global pandemics, etc., negatively impact the market, which may lower your returns too.

- **Credit Risk (Default Risk):** There is a risk that your borrower will default on a loan, bond, or other forms of debt, failing to make required payments.

- **Interest Rate Risk:** An investment's value can change due to a change in the absolute level of interest rates, especially for bonds.

- **Liquidity Risk:** There is a risk that you will not be able to buy or sell an investment quickly enough to prevent a loss or make a profit.

- **Inflation Risk (Purchasing Power Risk):** Inflation may erode the purchasing power of money, affecting the real returns on investments.
- **Currency Risk (Exchange Rate Risk):** This is a risk of loss from fluctuations in the exchange rate between two currencies, especially if you have purchased foreign stocks.
- **Concentration Risk:** This risk is associated with having a significant portion of an investment portfolio concentrated in a single investment, industry, or geographic area, which can lead to higher volatility.
- **Geopolitical Risk:** Political instability or changes in government policies may affect the value of investments.
- **Operational Risk:** The business you invest in is susceptible to fraud, business errors, and technical failures.
- **Reinvestment Risk:** There is a risk that cash flows from an investment will be reinvested at a lower rate of return. This is a common risk for bonds and other fixed-income investments when interest rates are falling.

Risk Management Strategies

While minimizing risks with diversification is a viable option, in most other cases, you will have to learn how to manage risks. The investment options open to you *at this age* don't carry much risk. Nevertheless, it is better to understand the fundamental types of risk management strategies. A fair warning: *you are entering advanced financial waters.*

- **Asset Allocation:** This involves distributing investments among different asset classes (stocks, bonds, real estate, etc.) according to your financial goals and risk tolerance. The correct asset allocation balances the risk and return of the portfolio (the selected collection of asset classes) by adjusting the proportion of each asset class.
- **Regular Portfolio Rebalancing:** Over time, the actual allocation of assets in a portfolio can drift from the original target allocation due to differing returns from each asset class. Regularly rebalancing the portfolio back to the target allocation helps maintain the desired level of risk. (Put more simply, your basket of goods has different performers; check it often to make sure the performers are performing as hoped!)

- **Use of Stop Loss Orders:** A stop-loss order is an order placed with a broker to buy or sell once the stock reaches a certain price. It is designed to limit your loss on a security position. Setting stop losses can automate the process of taking profits and cutting losses.

- **Hedging:** You can use financial instruments like *options* and *futures* to hedge against potential losses in your investment portfolio. (Imagine you have a collection of rare trading cards that you think will become more valuable over time. But you're worried that something might happen that makes them worth less instead. To protect your collection, you make a deal with a friend. If the value of your cards goes down, your friend will give you some money to make up for the loss. But if the value goes up, you might give your friend a little bit of your profit) Hedging involves taking an offsetting position in a related asset, which can help protect against losses due to adverse price movements. In other words, you bet for the "winner" but also place bets on possible "losers" because things can change!

- **Risk Assessment and Management Tools:** You can use financial tools and software that assess risk exposure and help you make informed decisions based on the risk profile of your investment portfolio.

- **Dollar-Cost Averaging (DCA):** Regardless of the investment's cost, a set quantity of money is routinely invested using this technique. Since DCA spreads out the cost of investments, it can eventually lessen the impact of volatility (the ups and downs) on the total purchase price of investments.

It is important to develop a disciplined approach to risk management that will contribute to an investment strategy that may move up and down at the market's whim. Ask yourself the following questions:

- What do I want to achieve with my investments?
- How much risk am I willing to tolerate?
- How much loss am I willing to take?
- How much profit do I think I can make without letting greed take over?

Creating an effective risk management strategy is just one of the many steps of investing for teens. Before investing in the asset of your choice, double-check online if there is an age limit. What are the rules for investing in it? What are the alternatives? Conduct extensive market research. If there is something you don't understand, clear your doubts by asking your parents or seeking help from a professional financial advisor.

Section 8: Turning Passion into Profit

The passion economy is livelier than ever before. The internet has made it a lot easier for you to make money from your interests. With minimal resources, people are growing profitable businesses because you no longer need a building to sell from, but you can create a professional storefront online. The beauty of monetizing your passions is that you can grow your business slowly while you are still in school. You do not have to wait and can start immediately.

The internet has made it a lot easier for you to make money from your interests.
https://www.pexels.com/photo/close-up-photography-of-smartphone-icons-267350/

A popular saying is that *if you do something you love, you'll never have to work a day in your life.* Pursuing a passion for making money allows you to dedicate yourself to what you like instead of getting trapped in the common cycle of tolerating a dreadful job because you need the money. If you lay the foundations of your passion now, by the time you graduate, you will have made a lot of progress toward your ultimate vision. Keep in mind that it is never too early to get started.

"Teenpreneurship"

"Teenpreneurship" is a play on the words "teen" and "entrepreneur." This is done to emphasize the fact that young people are making major moves! Technology has opened up the world in so many ways. From education to marketing, the online space is vibrant and packed with everything a start-up needs. With a simple laptop or smartphone, internet access, and an unwavering drive, you can start earning almost immediately. There is no such thing as an overnight success, so it will take a lot of hard work and commitment.

There is a misconception about entrepreneurship that many only learn once they begin. The idea of being your own boss is glamorized, giving teens the impression they have the freedom to do whatever they want. That is the opposite of the truth. As an entrepreneur, you will have much less time for fun because your idea will consume every bit of your free time. The responsibility of having to control every aspect of a business, as opposed to only one part of it as an employee, can be overwhelming. Before you explore the path of the entrepreneur, you must be certain that you are willing to make the sacrifices needed to succeed.

Exercise 1: Using the Internet to Learn

The journey toward entrepreneurship begins with knowledge. Once you have identified your passion, you will need to learn the skills required to take it to the next level. The first step to becoming great at something is to first completely suck at it. By emptying yourself and being open to learning, you are in the perfect position to excel. In modern times, you no longer need to join expensive schools or colleges to gain a new skill. The internet has tons of courses and free content you can use to improve on what you are passionate about.

Before you can sell something, it helps to reach a certain level of competence so your clients do not feel ripped off and will keep coming back for more. You will always be improving on your passion as long as you are working on it, but it helps pass a certain threshold before you present yourself to the market.

- List three things that you are passionate about.
- Which one of these are you the best at?
- Of the three, which one do you think you can create a business with?

Select one of these ideas, then go to YouTube and type in "Beginners course in..." followed by your passion. You will find several videos you can use to enhance your skills. Dedicate some time every day to improve until you are comfortable enough presenting it to the world.

Self-Reflection

Your teen years, and a lot of your twenties, will be spent trying to find where you fit in the world while developing the person you want to be. Discovering what you are passionate about can be hard; you're changing a lot. Self-reflection, then, is an essential concept for you to understand. Taking a good hard look at your passions will help you understand how and why you do what you do – and that makes your decisions more informed.

Exercise 2: Practical Self-reflection

Once you start pursuing your passion, you may run into a few obstacles. Self-reflection in these scenarios becomes a handy tool to unpack why these hurdles arise and how you can overcome them. When you are busy with a project or have completed a task, ask the following questions.

- What have I learned from completing the task?
- Which hurdles have I overcome?
- Which hurdles am I still struggling with – and why?
- What can I do differently?
- What do I know now that I didn't know before?
- Are there any changes I can make to ensure that I don't make the same mistakes – and how can I, in the future, implement the lessons I've learned?

Sometimes, to find what your passion is and how you can utilize it to make a profit, you need to reflect. You can use these questions to analyze your actions and mindset.

- What is important to me?
- What changes have I gone through recently?
- How can I align my actions more with what I value?
- How can I make money from my values?

Exercise 3: SWOT Analysis

SWOT ANALYSIS

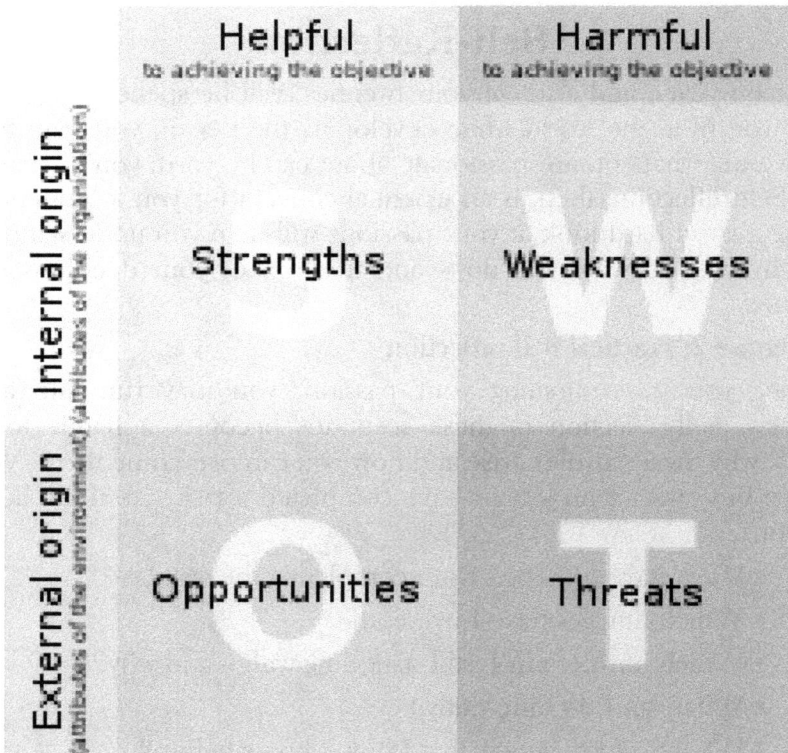

	Helpful to achieving the objective	Harmful to achieving the objective
Internal origin (attributes of the organization)	Strengths	Weaknesses
External origin (attributes of the environment)	Opportunities	Threats

SWOT stands for strengths, weaknesses, opportunities, and threats.
*Xhienne, CC BY-SA 2.5 <https://creativecommons.org/licenses/by-sa/2.5>, via Wikimedia
Commons: https://commons.wikimedia.org/wiki/File:SWOT_en.svg*

To turn your passion into a business, you need to understand you are operating in a competitive market. You should reflect on what you can bring to the market and what you can do to best serve your clients. A great way to do that is by using a SWOT analysis. SWOT stands for strengths, weaknesses, opportunities, and threats. Your strengths are what you are good at. Your weaknesses are your limitations. Opportunities are external forces you can use to generate income with your passion. Threats are the barriers in the way you make money with your passion.

- What business am I creating with your passion?
- What are its strengths?
- What are its weaknesses?
- What opportunities are there in the market?
- What threats are there in the market?

Simplified Business Plan Template

Business plans serve two main purposes. Primarily, it will give you an overview of your business, and secondly, it can be used as a tool to gain investment. A simple business plan of about two to three pages is perfect for both serving as the anchor of your vision and as a way to attempt to gain start-up funds. There are always programs looking to invest in young talent, so it helps to stay ready instead of trying to get ready. Creating a business plan can be useful in directing the path you follow to excel in your passion-based business, as well as being a blueprint you can present in fundraising situations.

Exercise 4: Business Plan

Follow this basic template for your business plan. Go into detail, and remember to keep your language precise.

Description: Include in the description the goals of your business, why it has been established, and how it is financed. Highlight any successes you have had, as well as obstacles you have managed to overcome.

Summary: This summary should include an overview as well as the basic branding of your business.

Product or Service: Describe the product or service you are offering in detail and how it will be unique in the market. Also, make sure that you outline how it benefits your clients.

Marketing Plan: Your marketing plan should include how you are going to introduce yourself to the market, as well as what will separate you from your competitors. It should also include how much you will sell within the next year or two and how you plan to achieve those numbers.

SWOT Analysis: Like the exercise you completed earlier in the chapter, this SWOT analysis should present the strengths of the business as well as how you plan to enhance them and the weaknesses and how you plan to address them too. It should also include opportunities, how to take advantage of them, threats, and how to overcome them.

Implementation: The implementation part of the document should be a detailed outline of every step of your business, from its creation to when it is mature enough in the market. You should consider how you will operate in all the stages of your business and how you will respond to any issues that arise.

Financial Plan: The financial plan is often considered the most critical part of a business plan. Here, you should outline how the business is going to be funded and how much income you will generate. It should also include a detailed budget that highlights all the money involved to keep the ship sailing.

Budgeting Principles

A budget is created before a single cent is spent. In the first two years of business, it is uncommon to immediately start making money. Most of the profits and income you generate should go back into the business in the early stages, so keep that in mind during your planning process.

There are five elements you need to know to create a solid and workable budget for your start-up.

- **Income:** This is the amount of money you generate monthly.
- **Fixed Expenses:** These are the costs of operating your business each month. For example, rent, electricity, and raw materials.
- **Debt:** This is money you owe on any loans you have made.
- **Flexible and Unplanned Expenses:** These are the costs in your business that change from month to month. For example, a business trip or emergency breakdowns.
- **Savings:** This is the money you put aside each month.

There are also three budget control principles you need to adhere to once you start spending. Sometimes, you can move away from the budget for a variety of reasons. Budgetary control means the steps you take to bring your spending back in line with your budget.

These are the three steps you need to take to promote budgetary control.

- Compare how much you've spent to how much you've planned to spend.
- Figure out why there are differences in spending.
- Take steps to bring spending back into the appropriate range.

Exercise 5: Creating a Budget for a Business

It feels amazing when you start making money from your passion. You may be tempted to spend every dime of the profit that you get once it starts flowing in, but this is the perfect way to fail. As an entrepreneur, your budget can make or break your business.

- How much does it cost to run your business?
- What are your plans for expansion, and what will it cost?
- How much profit do you currently make?
- How much profit do you want to make in a year?
- What steps will you take to ensure that growth?

Exercise 6: Investing and Expansion

In your business plan, you need to describe the ways you intend to grow your business as it progresses. You start small from one central point and expand outwards - just like if you were mining and expanding a hole in the ground. The best way to expand is by maxing out your sales capabilities and then moving outward toward related industries. For example, you start by cutting hair as a barber from your home. Then, you move into a shop, giving you space to employ more barbers. From there, you might employ some hairdressers, make-up artists, and nail techs. Then, you'll finally explore producing your own hair and beauty products. Notice how each step is related to the previous one in some way.

- Write down the business you have in mind based on your passion.
- Which other businesses are related to it?

- How can you expand it in a similar way as the barbershop example?

Basic Market Research

Passion alone is not enough to make money. You have to find a way your passion aligns with the market so you can serve the wants and needs of a target audience. This alignment requires market research. The first step in starting any successful business is by conducting effective research. You will need to understand your brand identity, as well as the competitors. You will also need to research how much money the entire market you are entering generates to calculate who has the biggest slice of the market and how big of a portion you are aiming for.

Exercise 7: Identifying Your Target Audience

Your target audience is the people to whom you are selling your product or service. They are divided according to demographics. Demographics are the different groups you can divide a population into, including age, race, gender, area, and income.

Do some research on the potential target audience for your business.

Fill in the details of each demographic factor to help you define your target audience.

- Age
- Gender
- Race
- Income
- Area
- Employment status
- Income level
- Educational status
- Political alignment
- Family structure

Exercise 8: Positioning and Branding

Positioning is how your product is related to your competitors in the market. For example, one toothpaste may market itself for sensitive teeth, another will focus on gum health, while another brand may be more aligned with children. You must figure out how your brand will fit into the market.

- Describe how you want your product or service to be viewed by people. Is it fun and exciting, or is it relaxed and smooth? Use about three to four sentences for the description. This is your brand identity.
- Research five to ten brands in the industry you want to enter.
- Describe their brand identities.
- Where will your brand fit into this environment, and what makes it unique?

Exercise 9: Networking

It is not always about what you know. Sometimes, it is about who you know. Networking is the process of getting to know people in your industry or related industries that can help you grow your business. You need to be in a position to provide something valuable to them so that they can give you the help you need.

- Go on Facebook, Instagram, Reddit, or any other social media website.
- Join groups or follow people related to the industry you want to join.
- Interact with these companies or people so that you can start making yourself known in the market.
- Remember to stay safe on the internet. Never meet with people you do not know or give out private information.

Teenage Success Stories

Destiny Snow is a brilliant entrepreneur who started her own business with $600 at the age of 15. Just two years later, she managed to grow her business exponentially, having made over $1 million in sales in two years. Destiny used her relatively large social media following to promote Snowglam Collection, a high-end fashion online store. Destiny emphasizes the need to keep studying and learning all you can. She attributes some of her success to her ability to understand social media and how to get engagement from her followers. She highlights that starting a business is difficult at first, but you need to constantly analyze your brand and make the necessary adjustments to keep moving forward. She has learned a lot from her mistakes and is now dedicated to helping other young entrepreneurs succeed.

Exercise 10: Reflection

- What about the above story inspires you?
- How can you recreate that to be relevant to your passion?
- What lessons can you learn from Destiny?
- What qualities of Destiny can you mimic?
- Outline a vision for what you would like your passion-based business to look like in the future.
- What work can you put in today to bring you closer to your goals?

Thank You Message

You've finally reached the finish line, but it is not close to over! This is just the beginning of your financial journey.

Thank you for the commitment and effort you have put into diligently working through all the aspects of financial literacy, including budgeting, saving, investing, and using your money wisely. Essentially, money is a tool, and when you know what to do with what you have, the potential of what you can build is endless. You have taken the first steps into a prosperous future by informing yourself. That is commendable in its own right because many will not reach this point.

However, there is still a lot of work to do. Your curiosity and courage to enter the world of money and finance communicate much about the type of person you are. Your ambition and organization indicate that you have what it takes to rise to the top, but you will have to put the work in. You need more than simply knowing the methods of working with money. You have to apply the techniques you learned in this book.

People who have managed to attain unimaginable wealth understand the intricacies of directing the flow of money to create desirable outcomes. Controlling the flow of money is directly tied to the choices you make. Your decisions will lead to abundance or pockets full of dust. Be wise when deciding how you use your money, and think about every penny you spend. Living in the moment with your money can be fun, but when you look back and realize that what you spent your hard-earned cash on did not serve you, your regret will multiply.

You will make mistakes but are still young enough to learn from them. Getting a head start on understanding money will assist you once you enter the workforce or begin actively competing in the brutal and oversaturated economy. The edge you get by learning early on will put you in a better position to understand things your peers have yet to study.

The techniques in this book will be helpful, but you need to get out into the field and start testing which methods work best for you. Through practical application, the details begin to unfold so that you can gain a deeper understanding of money and finance. Your responsibilities will grow as you age but learning how to manage money now will allow you to easily tackle any obstacles attached to money. Your work now may seem insignificant, but you can rest assured that you will gain a stable and comfortable lifestyle from learning how to correctly manage your money.

If you enjoyed this book, I'd greatly appreciate a review on Amazon because it helps me to create more books that people want. It would mean a lot to hear from you.

To leave a review:

1. Open your camera app.
2. Point your mobile device at the QR code.
3. The review page will appear in your web browser.

Thanks for your support!

Check out another book in the series

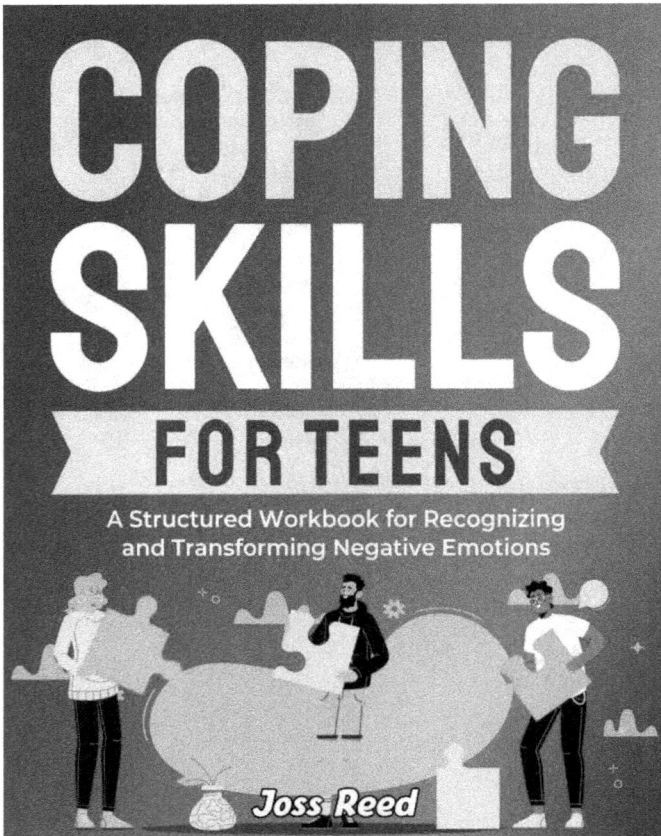

COPING SKILLS FOR TEENS

A Structured Workbook for Recognizing and Transforming Negative Emotions

Joss Reed

References

12 Tips to Balance Academics and Extracurricular Activities. (n.d.). Princeton Review. https://www.princetonreview.com/college-advice/12-tips-to-balance-academics-and-extracurriculars

Adams, D. (2023, December 6). How Old Do You Have To Be To Get A Credit Card? – Forbes Advisor. Forbes. https://www.forbes.com/advisor/credit-cards/how-old-do-you-have-to-be-to-get-a-credit-card

Allen, N. (2023, November 21). How to Make Money as a Teen. Investopedia. https://www.investopedia.com/how-to-make-money-as-a-teen-7550056

Baker, L. (n.d.). How Does Peer Pressure Influence Your Teen's Purchasing | Scripted. Scripted. https://www.scripted.com/writing-samples/how-does-peer-pressure-influence-your-teen-s-purchasing-choices

Baluch, A. (2022, July 14). How To Save Money as a Teenager. The Balance. https://www.thebalancemoney.com/how-to-save-money-as-a-teenager-5204306

Becker, J. (n.d.). 5 Reasons You Should Focus on Quality over Quantity. Haus von Eden. https://www.hausvoneden.com/lifestyle/5-reasons-why-you-should-focus-on-quality-instead-of-quantity/

Becker, S. (2023, November 7). 6 Investment Risk Management Strategies. SoFi. https://www.sofi.com/learn/content/investment-risk-management

Bennett, R. (2023, June 20). 5 Ways To Avoid Impulse Buying. Bankrate. https://www.bankrate.com/banking/savings/ways-to-avoid-impulse-buying/

Budgeting Basics: The 50-30-20 Rule. (n.d.). UNFCU. https://www.unfcu.org/financial-wellness/50-30-20-rule

Business Plan Template. (n.d.). https://www.knysna.gov.za/wp-content/uploads/2019/11/Business-plan-template.pdf

Carlson, S. (2022, October 25). How Delaying Gratification Can Help You Achieve Your Money Goals. LinkedIn. https://www.linkedin.com/pulse/how-delaying-gratification-can-help-you-achieve-your-sarah

Consumer Financial Protection Bureau. (n.d.). Teenagers and saving. Consumer Financial Protection Bureau. https://www.consumerfinance.gov/consumer-tools/money-as-you-grow/teen-young-adult/explore-saving/

Cruze, R. (2023, October 13). Impulse Buying: Why We Do It and How to Stop. Ramsey Solutions. https://www.ramseysolutions.com/budgeting/stop-impulse-buys

Dubey, S. (2023, July 27). The Impact of Social Media on Teen Spending Habits. Investor's Cabin. https://investorscabin.com/articles/the-impact-of-social-media-on-teen-spending-habits

Fay, B. (2018). The Emotional Effects of Debt - Denial, Stress, Fear, Depression. Debt. https://www.debt.org/advice/emotional-effects/

Fernando, J. (2023, March 30). What Is Financial Literacy, and Why Is It So

Important? Investopedia. https://www.investopedia.com/terms/f/financial-literacy.asp

Fry, R. (2014, May 14). Young Adults, Student Debt and Economic Well-Being. Pew Research Center's Social & Demographic Trends Project. https://www.pewresearch.org/social-trends/2014/05/14/young-adults-student-debt-and-economic-well-being

Geier, B. (2023, June 21). 11 Common Types of Investments and How They Work. SmartAsset. https://smartasset.com/investing/types-of-investment

GGI Insights. (2024, January 29). Impulse Buying: Understanding and Controlling Spontaneous Shopping. Gray Group International. https://www.graygroupintl.com/blog/impulse-buying

GGI Insights. (n.d.). Delayed Gratification: The Power of Now for Later. Gray Group International. https://www.graygroupintl.com/blog/delayed-gratification

Hall, M. (2023, September 17). Barter System vs. Currency System: What's the Difference? Investopedia. https://www.investopedia.com/ask/answers/061615/what-difference-between-barter-and-currency-systems.asp

Harvest Wealth Partners. (2021, March 11). What Are the 5 Basic Elements of a Budget? | Harvest Wealth Partners | Financial Planners Dyer. Www.harvestwp.com. https://www.harvestwp.com/what-are-the-5-basic-elements-of-a-budget/

How To Save Money As A Teenager - HSBC UK. (n.d.). Www.hsbc.co.uk. https://www.hsbc.co.uk/savings/how-to-save-money-as-a-teenager/

Indeed Editorial Team. (2023, January 30). 11 Job Interview Tips for Teens. Indeed. https://www.indeed.com/career-advice/interviewing/interview-tips-for-teens

Jain, P. (2022, May 14). 7 Reasons Why Teens Should Start Earning Money. LinkedIn. https://www.linkedin.com/pulse/7-reasons-why-teens-should-start-earning-money-payal-jain/

Lake, R. (2022, July 5). Budgeting for Teens: What You Need to Know. The Balance. https://www.thebalancemoney.com/how-to-teach-your-teen-about-budgeting-4160105

Mayerle, M. (2022, July 23). What Are the Negative Effects of Impulse Buying? CreditNinja. https://www.creditninja.com/blog/what-are-the-negative-effects-of-impulse-buying/

Metzner, M. (2022, October 24). Mindful Spending: 10 Simple Tips to Stay Financially Centered. Best Egg Personal Loans. https://www.bestegg.com/blog/mindful-spending/

Mint. (2022, June 30). Budgeting for Teens: 14 Tips for Growing Your Money Young. MintLife Blog. https://mint.intuit.com/blog/budgeting/budgeting-for-teens/

Modu, E. (2024, January 2). 7 Steps to Investing as a Teenager [in 2023]. TeenVestor. https://www.teenvestor.com/7steps

Money Management Tips for Teens. (n.d.). Credit Counselling Society. https://nomoredebts.org/budgeting/budgeting-for-teens

Money: Definition, Classification, Uses & Examples | StudySmarter. (n.d.). StudySmarter UK. https://www.studysmarter.co.uk/explanations/macroeconomics/financial-sector/money/

Morgan, K. (2023, December 11). Mindful Spending: How to Stop Spending Money on Unnecessary Things. Unbiased. https://www.unbiased.co.uk/discover/personal-finance/budgeting/mindful-spending-how-to-stop-spending-money-on-unnecessary-things

Naik, A. (2023, November 22). How to Stop Your Teen from Impulsive Spending. GoHenry. https://www.gohenry.com/uk/blog/financial-education/how-to-stop-your-teen-from-impulsive-spending

Napoletano, E. (2020, July 28). What Is Investing? How Can You Start Investing? Forbes. https://www.forbes.com/advisor/investing/what-is-investing

Peintner, L. (2020, January 8). 5 Self-Reflection Exercises to Start Your Year Off Right. Www.idealist.org. https://www.idealist.org/en/careers/5-self-reflection-exercises

Perna, M. C. (2022, March 2). At 15, This Entrepreneur Started A Business With $600. 2 Years Later, She's Worth $1 Million. Forbes.
https://www.forbes.com/sites/markcperna/2022/03/02/at-15-this-entrepreneur-started-a-business-with-600-2-years-later-shes-worth-1-million/?sh=542719b83617

Perry, E. (2022, February 2). 13 Tips to Become a Successful Entrepreneur. Www.betterup.com. https://www.betterup.com/blog/entrepreneur-tips

Princeton University. (2016, May 16). Choose a Job You Love, and You Will Never Have to Work a Day in Your Life. Philosophy. https://philosophy.princeton.edu/news/choose-job-you-love-and-you-will-never-have-work-day-your-life

Rakoczy, C. (2019, April 2). Why Money Is Important: Benefits, Downsides, and More. LendEDU. https://lendedu.com/blog/why-money-is-important/

Responsible Borrowing. (n.d.). Look Forward to Your Future. https://lookforwardwi.gov/responsible-borrowing

Risk and Return: Examples & Types | StudySmarter. (n.d.). StudySmarter UK. https://www.studysmarter.co.uk/explanations/macroeconomics/financial-sector/risk-and-return

Santander. (2023, February 1). What Are Central Banks and Why Are They So Important? Santander. https://www.santander.com/en/stories/what-is-a-central-bank

Sharkey, S. (2022, May 3). Financial Literacy for Teenagers: Key Money Tips For Teens. Clever Girl Finance. https://www.clevergirlfinance.com/financial-literacy-for-teenagers/

Simdev. (2017, May 5). Types of Investment Risk. GetSmarterAboutMoney.ca. https://www.getsmarteraboutmoney.ca/learning-path/understanding-risk/types-of-investment-risk

Staples, A. (2022, August 12). 4 Things Your Teenager Should Know About Money. Bankrate. https://www.bankrate.com/banking/checking/things-teenagers-should-know-about-money/

Teen Spending Plan. (n.d.). https://globalyouth.wharton.upenn.edu/wp-content/uploads/2015/12/Teen-Spending-Plan.pdf

Teens - 10 Tips on Smart Spending. (n.d.).
https://www.td.com/content/dam/tdb/document/pdf/personal-banking/teenssmartspendingtips-en.pdf

The Power of Delayed Gratification: A Key to Financial Well-Being. (2023, June 2).
Sort My Money. https://sortmymoney.com.au/the-power-of-delayed-gratification-a-key-to-financial-well-being/

Top Ten Shopping Tips | Shop Your Wardrobe. (n.d.). Shopyourwardrobe.com.
https://shopyourwardrobe.com/top-ten-shopping-tips/

TWK Admin. (2019, November 29). Shopping Tips for Teens Looking to Get the Most Out of the Season. Teens Wanna Know. https://teenswannaknow.com/shopping-tips-for-teens-looking-to-get-the-most-out-of-the-season/

V., S. (2023, September 19). How Delaying Gratification Can Lead You To a Wealthy Life. Www.linkedin.com. https://www.linkedin.com/pulse/how-delaying-gratification-can-lead-you-wealthy-life-saniya-v-

Volopay. (n.d.). What are the 5 Steps of Budgetary Control Process? Volopay.
https://www.volopay.com/expense-management/budgetary-control-process/

What Are the Benefits of Long-Term Investing? (2023, October 12). Wealthify.
https://www.wealthify.com/blog/what-are-the-benefits-of-long-term-investing.

What Are the Different Types of Consumer Debt? (n.d.). Equifax.
https://www.equifax.com/personal/education/debt-management/articles/-/learn/types-of-consumer-debts

What Is Mindful Spending? – HSBC UK. (n.d.). Www.hsbc.co.uk.
https://www.hsbc.co.uk/sustainability/mindful-spending/

Whiteman, L. (2024, January 12). How to Start Investing as a Teenager. The Motley Fool. https://www.fool.com/investing/how-to-invest/investing-for-teens

Woodard, D. (2022, August 30). Tips for Back-to-School Shopping With Teens. The Balance. https://thebalancemoney.com/tips-for-back-to-school-shopping-with-teens-6504780#toc-dont-forget-those-coupons-and-apps

www.ingramcontent.com/pod-product-compliance
Lightning Source LLC
Chambersburg PA
CBHW060034050426

42448CB00012B/3008